PARABLES
to Learn By

PARABLES
to Learn By

Based on Stories Told by Jesus

Written by Bob Hartman

Illustrated by Terry Julien

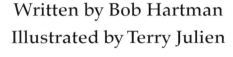

Pauline
BOOKS & MEDIA
Boston

Library of Congress Cataloging-in-Publication Data

Hartman, Bob, 1955–
   Parables to learn by: based on stories told by Jesus / written by Bob Hartman; illustrated by Terry Julien.
      p. cm.
   ISBN 0-8198-5933-8 (pbk.)
   1. Jesus Christ—Parables—Juvenile literature. [1. Jesus Christ—Parables. 2. Parables. 3. Bible stories—
N.T.] I. Julien, Terry, ill. II. Title.
   BT367 .H37 2001
   226.8'09505—dc21

2001001927

Life applications, questions and prayers were written by Patricia Edward Jablonski, FSP, based on ideas contributed by Mary Elizabeth Tebo, FSP.

Scripture quotations in this publication are from the *Holy Bible: Contemporary English Version.* Copyright © American Bible Society, 1995. Used by permission.

Printed and published in the U.S.A. by Pauline Books & Media, 50 Saint Pauls Avenue, Boston, MA 02130-3491.

www.pauline.org

Pauline Books & Media is the publishing house of the Daughters of St. Paul, an international congregation of women religious serving the Church with the communications media.

1 2 3 4 5 6

06 05 04 03 02 01

Contents

A Note to Parents and Teachers

The parables were stories Jesus told that taught lessons about God and his kingdom by using familiar comparisons from everyday life. Each of Jesus' parables also included an element that caught his listeners by surprise. The stories made people stop and think. They challenged their hearers to make choices that could be acted upon.

Parables to Learn By is a collection of contemporary parables for children. Building on a theme from one of the parables of Jesus, each story is followed by life application questions, the text of the actual Gospel parable, and a concluding prayer.

It is our hope that these stories will help children begin to discover "the secret about God's kingdom" (Mk 4:11), because, as Jesus said, "The kingdom of God belongs to people who are like these little children" (Mk 10:14).

The Editors

Solid as a Rock

Based on the Parable of the House Built on Rock

H ere we are!" shouted Counselor Ken. "The shores of Lake Minnietango."

He slipped off his knapsack and dropped it onto the sandy beach. "And this looks like the perfect spot to set up camp!"

Counselor Ken was a nice guy. One of the nicest that any of the kids had ever met. He was fun and enthusiastic and encouraging. But he knew nothing at all about camping. Everybody knew that. Well, everybody but Counselor Ken.

"Excuse me," interrupted Counselor Carol. "Don't you think it might be a bit safer to pitch our tents a little higher up? On the top of that hill, for instance?"

"Don't be silly," laughed Counselor Ken. "This spot is beautiful! We can jump in the lake whenever we like. And besides, I think we're all a little too tired to climb that hill just now." He looked at the boys in his group. "Right, men?"

The boys were tired. And hungry. And hot. A swim sounded good to them. So they nodded their heads in agreement.

"Well, if it's all the same to you," replied Counselor Carol, "I'll be taking my girls up the hill. Come along, ladies."

And although they were tired and hot and hungry, too, the girls followed. Counselor Carol knew what she was doing.

U p the steep hill the girls climbed. But as they went they couldn't help glancing back at the boys, who were already playing in the lake.

"At-ten-tion, men!" shouted

2

Counselor Ken. "Before we engage in any further recreational activities…"

"Fun stuff!" hollered one of the boys.

"…we must pitch our tents and gather firewood. In short, set up our camp."

"AWWW," the boys moaned, all at once.

But Counselor Ken was firm. "It will take no time at all," he assured them. "Trust me."

And that was just the case! The sand was so soft that it took no effort at all to push in the tent pegs. There was plenty of driftwood scattered about for their fire. And so, in less than half an hour, the boys were splashing about in the lake once again.

"Hey," one of the boys whispered to the others, "I think Counselor Ken knows something about camping, after all."

The girls, meanwhile, had only just arrived at the top of the hill. It took them ages to hammer their tent pegs into the hard, rocky ground. And they had to chop down every bit of wood they needed for their campfire.

"Why aren't we pitching camp down there with the boys?" groaned one of the girls.

Counselor Carol cast a worried look at the sky. "Because I think we're in for a storm tonight. And we're much safer up here. I know this is hard work, but you'll just have to trust me. I'll tell you what, though. When we're finished, we can go down and do some swimming ourselves."

And so they did. And when they had finished, the boys invited them to their campfire for ghost stories and s'mores and thirty-seven choruses of *Kumbaya.*

As the girls were packing up to leave, Counselor Carol turned to Counselor Ken one last time. "I really think you should consider joining us up on the hill. Those clouds look awfully mean."

"But we're already set up down here!" exclaimed Counselor Ken. "You can't expect the boys to tear down camp and set up all over again. It's late. And besides, I've already promised them a swim first thing in the morning."

"All right," sighed Counselor Carol, and she led her girls back up the hill. They tramped and they tripped and they trudged. By the time they reached their camp, they were ready to fall into their sleeping bags. They were so tired that they didn't even notice it had started to rain.

First there was a drizzle.
Then came a steady downpour.
And finally, the thunder and the lightning and the wind announced that this was going to be a serious storm.

But the girls didn't pay any attention. Their tents were secure, pegged tight in the rocky ground. And so they slept,

warm and dry and dreaming of new adventures.

Counselor Carol slept, too. And she would have slept the whole night long, if she hadn't heard the cries for help coming from outside her tent.

When she poked her head through the flap, there were Counselor Ken and his boys, tired and cold and wet from head to toe.

"Pegs pulled out!"

"Tents flew off!"

"Sleeping bags in the lake!"

The story poured out all at once — a flood of words from sad, dripping faces.

"All right," mumbled Counselor Carol. "Let me see what I can do."

She woke the girls and, after much persuasion, convinced them to double up in half the tents, so the boys could use the others. She collected as many extra blankets as she could find, and soon the boys were as snug and as warm as could be expected.

Counselor Ken helped her, of course. But he was very, very quiet.

"So," she said to him at last, "are you still planning on that swim at the beach in the morning?"

"No," he answered, shaking his soggy head. "I think my boys and I have had as much sand and water as we can take for a long, long time."

Which of the two counselors made the wisest choice about the location of the campsite?

Where would *you* have pitched the tents if you had been in charge of the campers?

6

Jesus once told a story something like this one. It was about a wise builder and a foolish builder. Jesus used his story to teach the people that his *true* follower is the person who not only listens to his words, but also puts them into practice.

Here is Jesus' story:

Two Builders
(Mt 7:24–27)

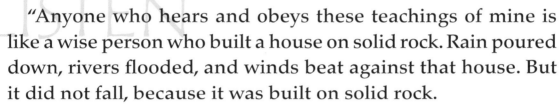

"Anyone who hears and obeys these teachings of mine is like a wise person who built a house on solid rock. Rain poured down, rivers flooded, and winds beat against that house. But it did not fall, because it was built on solid rock.

"Anyone who hears my teachings and doesn't obey them is like a foolish person who built a house on sand. The rain poured down, the rivers flooded, and the winds blew and beat against that house. Finally, it fell with a crash."

In this Gospel story the solid rock that the first man builds his house on stands for Jesus' words and teachings. These teachings reveal what God our Father wants us to do.

What do you think the rain, the floods and the wind in the story stand for?

Jesus, I want to be your follower. I believe all that you've told us in the Gospels. Help me to obey and put your teachings into practice!

Garage Sale

*Based on the Parables of the Hidden Treasure
and the Valuable Pearl*

Josh couldn't figure it out. Rain was dripping in his ear. Wind was blowing through his light brown jacket. It was a murky and muddy and miserable autumn day. But no one in the crowd around him seemed to notice at all.

They sorted through bundles of second-hand socks. They rummaged through wrecks of old radios and cassette players. They argued over ugly old knickknacks. It was the season's final garage sale. And Josh hated it!

But what choice did he have? He'd spent the night with his best friend, Logan. And Logan's mom was seriously into garage sales. So where was Josh? He was stuck here with soggy feet and soggy clothes and soggy hair. He sighed a soggy sigh and splashed around through piles of junk.

The toys were no good. They were either broken or really out of date. He wasn't interested in the collection of 8-bit computer games or any of the sports equipment. And there were no baseball cards that even a beginning collector would have paid money for. So he shuffled through stacks of old records and rows of creepy ceramic cats, trying hard to avoid that chubby woman with the "break-it-you-buy-it" eyes.

And that's when he saw the chest of drawers. There were stains down the front and perfectly round footprints of coffee cups on the top. Along the sides hung the ragged remains of old stickers that the owner had not been able to scrape completely off.

Josh opened the top drawer and looked inside. Nothing.

The second drawer was empty, too.

And the third drawer — well, he almost didn't bother opening it at all. But when Josh saw Logan's mom arguing over the price of a bathroom mat, he pulled the third drawer slowly open.

Just as it started to move, however, he heard a scraping sound from underneath — as if something was stuck. He did it again, and — sure enough — there was the sound again. Josh was curious now, so he gave the drawer a powerful tug and pulled it all the way out. Underneath where the drawer had been, there was an old baseball card, caught in the corner of the chest.

Now Josh was *really* curious. Suddenly the cold and the rain didn't matter anymore. He stuck his head in the drawer space as far as it would go. But that only blocked out the light. So he shoved the drawer halfway in and hurried over to a pile of flashlights he'd seen before. He found one that

worked, then rushed back to the chest of drawers.

Someone else was looking at it!

"It's all scratched," he said to the lady who had come over. "And, look," he added, pulling on the third drawer, "it's kind of stuck."

"Hmm," the woman muttered, and moved on.

Then Josh pulled that third drawer all the way out and shone the flashlight into the corner.

He could hardly believe what he saw!

Henry Aaron was on that card. Henry Aaron the slugger. Henry Aaron the Hall of Famer. Henry Aaron — the rookie! It was a genuine, original Hank Aaron rookie card, worth hundreds, maybe thousands of dollars!

Josh reached out a trembling hand.

"And what exactly are you doing, young man? These things are for sale. They're not for playing with!" It was the chubby woman.

Josh froze. He didn't know what to do. He felt pretty stupid with his head stuck in the chest. But he didn't want to move, either, and take the risk of her discovering the treasure hidden in the corner of her old piece of furniture.

"I'm...um...just looking at that old...um...chest of drawers," he mumbled. "I...I need something like this for my room." He was trying to sound believable, so he asked the most obvious question he could think of. "Could you tell me how much you want for this?"

"A hundred bucks!" the woman grunted. "And not a penny less. It's an antique, after all. Now get out of there before you break it!"

Josh muttered back an "OK" and grabbed the card. But it was stuck — pinched between the back and the side of the chest. There was no way to get it out without ripping it. And that meant just one thing — if Josh

wanted that card, he was going to have to buy the chest of drawers!

What could he do? Any of the people there might decide to buy the chest, at any time. He couldn't tell Logan or Logan's mom. They'd probably want the treasure for themselves. So Josh made the only choice any self-respecting fourth grader would — he decided to be a pest.

"Uh, Mrs. Johnson," he whined to Logan's mom. "Uh, Mrs. Johnson, I'm really cold and wet and tired, and I think I might be coming down with the flu or something."

"All right, Joshua," she answered, her eyes glued to a cracked mirror with a fancy frame. "We'll be leaving any minute, now."

Josh knew perfectly well what that phrase meant.

"But, Mrs. Johnson, I can't wait that long," he sniffled. "My stomach feels really bad, too. And the last time I felt like this —" Josh blew out his cheeks and tried to look as green as possible.

It did the trick! In five minutes, Josh and Logan were belted into the back seat of the Johnson minivan, headed off for home. Josh staggered up his driveway and into the front door. But the minute he got inside, he ran to his mom and told her the whole story.

"That's very exciting, Josh," she said, "but I don't have a hundred dollars to spend, even on a valuable baseball card. Besides, I can't imagine you wanting to sell it once you got it, anyway."

She was right, of course. But there had to be a way to get that card. Josh trudged up the stairs to his room. As he looked around the answer came. Why not have a garage sale of his own?

Not a real garage sale — there wasn't time for that. But he did have things — valuable things — that his friends would be sure to give him money for! He dug a big box out of the basement, and in twenty minutes it was loaded with computer games and videos and toys and baseball gloves — anything he could lay his hands on. Even his very best stuff.

Up and down the street Josh went, knocking on one friend's

door after another. It was hard, at first, selling his best stuff for far less than he knew it was worth. So he just kept thinking about Hank Aaron's face and what that rare and amazing card would mean for his baseball card collection. Finally, the box was empty. But his pockets were full of cash — a hundred dollars, at least!

Josh's mom drove him back to the garage sale. She understood — she really did — how important a card like this could be to him.

Josh raced up the driveway, past the chubby woman. But when he got to the place where the chest had been standing, it was gone!

"Where's that chest of drawers?" he cried. "The one that was right here!"

"On the back of that truck, over there," smirked the chubby woman. "That's what you get for waiting, kid."

Josh ran to the pickup truck. The woman who had been looking at the old chest before had just climbed behind the steering wheel.

"Wait!" Josh shouted. "Please wait! I want to buy that chest of drawers." By this time, Josh's mom had joined him. She could see that he was upset.

The woman in the truck rolled down her window. "I'm sorry," she mumbled. "You're too late."

"But it took me time to get the money," Josh moaned. "A hundred dollars is a lot!"

"Did you say a hundred dollars?" the woman asked. "Well, now that I know you wanted it so badly, I suppose I could let you have it."

"Thanks," Josh sighed. "This is really nice of you."

The woman opened her driver's door, and Josh counted one hundred dollars into her hand. Josh's mom helped him lift the chest down off the truck. Then the chubby woman piped up.

"Not a bad deal, I'd say," she chuckled to the lady in the truck. "You buy that chest for twenty bucks and sell it for a hundred, ten minutes later."

The woman in the truck looked a little embarrassed. Josh looked like he was going to cry.

"Twenty?" he sputtered. "But you told me a hundred!"

"This is a garage sale, kid. You always start high and then take what you can get. But it's too late now. A deal's a deal."

"That's right," agreed Josh's mom, as she pulled out the bottom drawer and peered into the corner of the old chest. "Oh, look, honey. Here's that baseball card you were telling me about. What did you say it was worth?"

"It's a *real* Hank Aaron rookie card." Josh grinned. "And it could be worth as much as a thousand dollars."

"What?" moaned the woman in the truck.

"What?" echoed the chubby woman. "Give me that!"

"Oh, no," said Josh's mom firmly. "Just like you said, 'a deal's a deal.'"

Then Josh and his mom loaded the chest into their station wagon and drove off smiling in the autumn rain.

Maybe garage sales weren't so bad after all.

Think of something that you'd *really* like to have, something that's as valuable to you as the Hank Aaron card was to Josh in this story. What would you be willing to give up or do to get this "treasure"?

Jesus taught us that the kingdom of heaven is the greatest treasure we could ever want. Living in the kingdom of heaven means living happily forever with God!

Jesus has left us some Gospel stories about the kingdom of heaven.

Here are two of them:

A Hidden Treasure *(Mt 13:44)*

LISTEN

"The kingdom of heaven is like what happens when someone finds a treasure hidden in a field and buries it again. A person like that is happy and goes and sells everything in order to buy that field."

A Valuable Pearl *(Mt 13:45-46)*

"The kingdom of heaven is like what happens when a shop owner is looking for fine pearls. After finding a very valuable one, the owner goes and sells everything in order to buy that pearl."

THINK

We can't "buy" heaven, but we can try to always please God, who wants to share heaven with all his followers. What are some ways that you can please God? What do you think heaven will be like?

PRAY

Jesus, there are so many things that I like and wish I could have. But not even all the money in the world can buy the greatest treasure. That treasure is the kingdom of heaven. Heaven is a gift, but I can prepare to receive it by being your loving disciple. Please help me to be loving just like you, Jesus.

Grounded!

Based on the Parable of the Unforgiving Official

Okay, it's not the worst day of my life. But it's pretty close. My family is out sledding — even my clumsy little sister. My friends have gone ice skating. And I'm stuck here in my room — grounded! — with nothing to look at but the broken pieces of the best Star Trek model ever.

The Klingons couldn't have done a better job of it. Or the Cardassians, either. There are chunks of the Enterprise everywhere! And it's all my stupid sister's fault. But is she sitting in her room? NOOO! She's flying down Miller's Hill — on my toboggan, probably — screaming and shouting and having all kinds of fun. And, like I said, I'm stuck in here.

All right, so maybe I shouldn't have been playing with my basketball in the house. But I was bored!

Dad was shoveling snow. Mom was up in the attic. And Kirsten was in her room, playing dolls or something. There was nothing on TV, so I was just dribbling on the wood floor downstairs. Chucking the ball in the air and catching it. Trying to spin it on my finger. You know, just goofing around. But somehow the ball kind of got away from me, and bounced across the room, and knocked that fancy lamp off the end table.

It was an ugly lamp, anyway. And it was old! It used to belong to my great-grandmother or something, and my dad is always making fun of it. But my mom loved that lamp, and as soon as she heard the crash she came tearing down the stairs.

She looked at the lamp. She looked at the basketball. She

looked at me. I thought I was dead for sure. Then she took a deep breath and said, very slowly, "Kevin, I want you to get the broom."

I took off at warp speed and swept up every broken piece.

"I'm sorry," I said.

"It was an accident," I said.

"I'll buy you another one," I said.

But my mom didn't say a thing. She waited till I was done, then she sat me down on the couch beside her.

Here it comes, I thought.

"Kevin," she said, "the lamp you broke was very old and valuable. It would cost at least a thousand dollars to replace it, and that's assuming I could find another one like it." I started to feel cold and sweaty all over. *Where would I ever get the money?* "No, you don't have to buy me another one," my mother said as if she could read my mind, "because there is no way you could. What I want you to do instead is to be more careful in the future, and to play your ball-games outside, where they're supposed to be played. Is that understood?"

I nodded. Well, what else could I do? And then I waited for the punishment.

"That's all," she said. "Now go help your father shovel the snow."

I couldn't believe my luck!

I did that warp speed thing again, putting on my coat and hat and gloves, but by the time I got outside, Dad was almost done. So I chucked a few snowballs at him and went back in for lunch.

And that's when my clumsy little sister decided to spoil the whole day!

I was coming down the hall, when I heard this noise in my room. Nobody's supposed to be in my room. Nobody but me. So I ran in there, warp speed again, and found my sister looking in one of my desk drawers.

"Hey!" I shouted. "Get out of there!" And instead of just shutting the drawer and leaving, she jumped like she was scared or something. And when she jumped, she banged into my model shelf, and knocked the U.S.S. Enterprise onto the floor.

I bought it with my own money! It took me ages to build! And there it was, in a million pieces, on the floor.

Oh, she said she was sorry. She was just looking for scissors or something. But she shouldn't have been in my room in the first place! And she shouldn't have been so clumsy. And now she was going to pay.

So I chased her, that's all. Out of my room and down the stairs and across the living room.

"When I'm done with you," I shouted, "you'll never come in my room again!"

And that's when we ran into my mom.

"K-e-v-i-n! K-i-r-s-t-e-n!" she hollered. "What's the matter with you two?"

23

But before I could say anything, Kirsten started crying about how I was going to hit her and how it was just an accident, anyway.

"She broke my model!" I yelled back. "And she was sneaking around in my room!" But it didn't do any good. Kirsten was hanging onto my mom like I was some kind of monster or something.

"Kevin," my mom said quietly, "earlier today, you broke something that belonged to me. Something that was very precious. Did I scream at you or threaten you? No. As a matter of fact, you weren't even punished.

"Half an hour later, your sister breaks one of your things, and look what you do. I know that model was special to you, but it would have cost very little to replace. I think you could have shown Kirsten just a little of the patience and kindness I tried to show you."

"But, Mom..." I said.

"No, Kevin. No 'buts.' Go to your room. And spend some time thinking about the way you treat others and the way you want to be treated."

So here I am. Stuck in my room. Thinking. And I still don't get it. I mean, just because my mom let me off the hook, does that mean I have to do the same for my sister...?

Can you think of a time when someone forgave you for doing something that hurt or bothered them, even if it was just an accident?

Can you think of a time when you refused to forgive someone who did something that hurt or bothered you, even if it was just an accident?

Jesus taught us that God our Father wants us to forgive, even when it's not easy.

Here's a great story Jesus once told about forgiveness:

An Official Who Refused to Forgive
(Mt 18:21–35)

Peter came up to the Lord and asked, "How many times should I forgive someone who does something wrong to me? Is seven times enough?"

Jesus answered:

"Not just seven times, but seventy-seven times! This story will show you what the kingdom of heaven is like:

"One day a king decided to call in his officials and ask them to give an account of what they owed him. As he was doing this, one official was brought in who owed him fifty million silver coins. But he didn't have any money to pay what he owed. The king ordered him to be sold, along with his wife and children and all he owned, in order to pay the debt.

"The official got down on his knees and began begging, 'Have pity on me, and I will pay you every cent I owe!' The king felt sorry for him and let him go free. He even told the official that he did not have to pay back the money.

"As the official was leaving, he happened to meet another official, who owed him a hundred silver coins. So he grabbed the man by the throat. He started choking him and said, 'Pay me what you owe!'

25

"The man got down on his knees and began begging, 'Have pity on me, and I will pay you back.' But the first official refused to have pity. Instead, he went and had the other man put in jail until he could pay what he owed.

"When some other officials found out what had happened, they felt sorry for the man who had been put in jail. Then they told the king what had happened. The king called the first official back in and said, 'You're an evil man! When you begged for mercy, I said you did not have to pay back a cent. Don't you think you should show pity to someone else, as I did to you?' The king was so angry that he ordered the official to be tortured until he could pay back everything he owed. That is how my Father in heaven will treat you, if you don't forgive each of my followers with all your heart."

In Jesus' story, the king stands for God and the officials stand for us.

How many times has God forgiven you when you've done something wrong and then told him that you're sorry? You've probably lost count.

Whenever you find it hard to forgive someone else, try to remember how kind and forgiving God has been with you, especially in the sacrament of Reconciliation.

Jesus, I know that you want me to always forgive others. But sometimes it's hard. I can't do it on my own, so please help me when the time comes. Thank you for all the times you've forgiven me!

Payday Problem

Based on the Parable of the Workers in a Vineyard

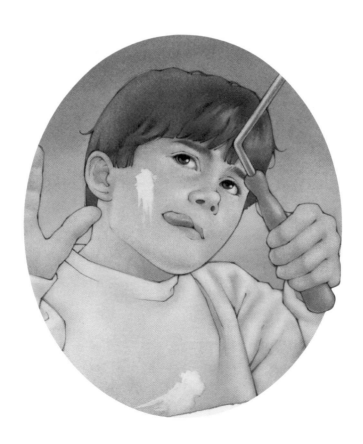

Bleep-beep" went the cash register.

"That will be ninety-seven cents," yawned Marsha, as she fixed her tired eyes on twelve-year-old Stephen. She'd been up much too late the night before, and 9:00AM seemed way too early for any sensible human being to have to be at work.

Stephen waited for the change, then tucked the morning paper under his arm, and shoved the pack of mini-donuts into his pocket. But just as he was leaving the Quick-Stop Mart, he bumped into Tony Shepherd.

Tony ran the Drop-in Center across the street from the Quick-Stop. Stephen and his friends hung out there sometimes, playing pool or Ping-Pong, or just reading old comics.

"Stephen!" Tony said, all out of breath. "Stephen, I'm really glad I bumped into you! The church group that was supposed to come and paint the recreation room today canceled out on me. But it has to be done for our Open House tomorrow. Is there any chance you could round up a few of your friends and help me out?"

Stephen fidgeted. He liked the Drop-in Center. And he liked Tony. But he didn't like painting at all. And besides, there was still a Saturday morning's worth of cartoons to watch.

"Look," Tony continued, "I'm desperate. I'll pay you ten dollars apiece if you work the whole day."

Stephen's expression changed. Painting was one thing. Ten bucks was another! Just the little extra he

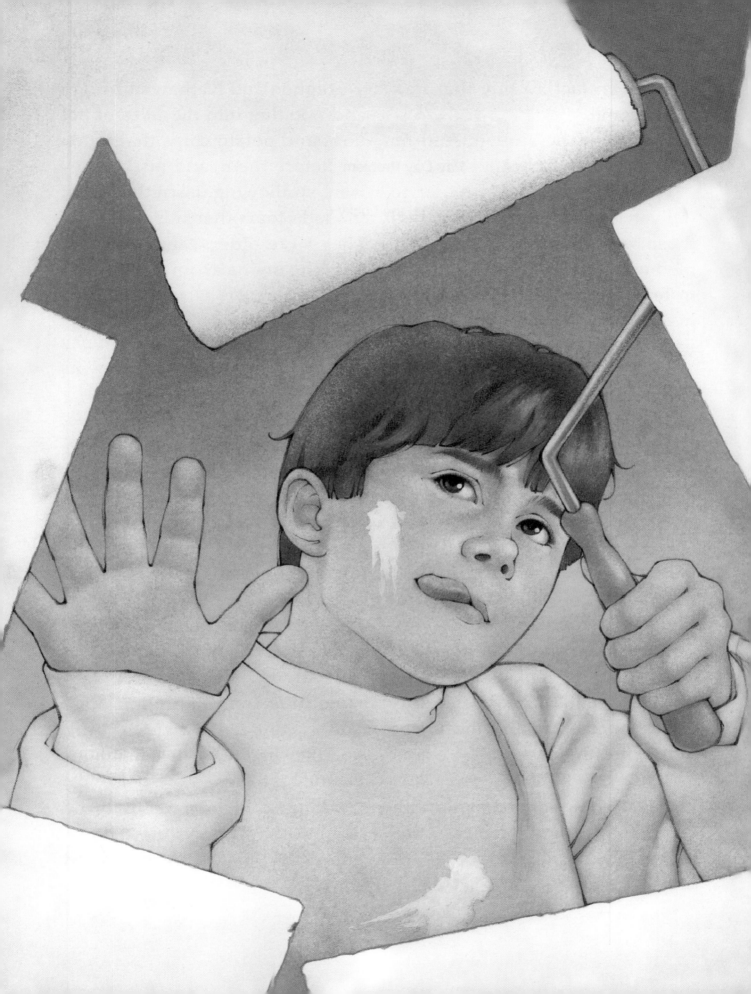

needed, in fact, to buy that new video game.

"I'll do it," he agreed. And he rushed off to find his friends.

There was his dad's paper to deliver first, of course, and then those breakfast donuts were gobbled up on the run from Nathan's to Brian's to Boo's. It was only at his last stop, in fact, that Stephen had any trouble.

"Just ten?" said Sammy, in disbelief. "I can get ten bucks from my dad whenever I want. I'd rather watch TV."

The work wasn't hard at all. Just messy. But Tony had spread drop cloths all over the stuff in the room and pushed it all to the middle. Tony's wife, Linda, was there, too, and every now and then she'd come around with soda and cookies and cake. Stephen and his friends painted as fast as they could, but when lunchtime came, there was still a whole lot left to do.

"We're going to need some more help," Tony sighed. "You boys finish your lunch, and I'll see what I can do."

Stephen and Nathan and Brian and Boo dug into the piles of hot dogs and potato chips that Linda set before them, and just as they were swallowing down the last of the soda, four other kids walked in. They were older: Mark and Ben and the twins from across the bridge.

What'd Tony say he'd pay us?" one of the twins asked Mark.

"He didn't say," Mark answered, loud enough for the younger boys to hear. "But he'll take care of us. Tony's a good guy."

Stephen looked at his friends and grinned. He knew one thing for sure. It wasn't going to be ten bucks!

The two groups kind of ignored each other, but the work went on well, anyway. Until Mark said something that made Ben mad. And a paint can got kicked over. And they had to waste a half hour cleaning it all up.

When six o'clock finally came around, they were almost done. And that's when Sammy showed up.

"Sammy, Sammy!" called Tony, like he was greeting his best friend. "Sammy, we only have an hour till the Center opens. We have to finish the painting and get the place straightened out. Is there any chance you could help?"

"Sure," Sammy said. "And there are a couple of girls over at the Quick-Stop who can help, too." Sammy ran to get them, and for the next hour everyone worked as hard as they'd worked all day. By the time the clock showed 7:00, the Center was ready.

Thanks, everybody." Tony smiled wearily. "Thanks a lot. We couldn't have done this without you. Stay as long as you like, but before you leave, be sure and see Linda. She'll give you your pay."

Stephen and his friends stopped at the Quick-Stop on the way home and opened up the envelopes Linda had given them. There was a crisp ten dollar bill inside each one.

"Wow! That's pretty good!" said Nathan. "Ten bucks and all the cookies and candy you can eat."

"I'll say," agreed another voice. But the voice didn't belong to Stephen or Brian or Boo. It came from behind the snack food shelves.

"I told the guys Tony would take care of us," smiled Mark, as he rounded the corner. "And ten bucks for a couple hours' work isn't all that bad."

Stephen and his friends looked at each other. But before any of them could holler "Unfair!" Mark walked out the door. "See you later, little guys," he called over his shoulder.

"Well, they *were* bigger than us," admitted Brian.

"And they didn't eat as many cakes," added Boo.

"That doesn't matter!" yelled Stephen. "We worked twice as long! All they should have gotten was five bucks."

"You kids found what you want?" asked Marsha.

The boys nodded, paid for their snacks, and headed for home. Outside, they met Sammy, who was just leaving the Drop-in Center. Stephen was still fuming about the pay the older boys had received. Maybe that's why he turned to Sammy and said, "Bet you're sorry you didn't come with us this morning."

Sammy looked at him sadly, "Yeah, I am."

Stephen turned and smiled at the others.

"If I got ten bucks for working just one hour," Sammy continued, "you guys must have made a fortune!"

"WHAT?" the four friends shouted together.

"Ten bucks," Sammy said. "I got ten bucks. Why? What did Tony pay you?"

Stephen and his friends marched back to the Drop-in Center, right then and there, leaving Sammy standing alone in the middle of the street. But when they got there, the door was locked.

Nothing was going to stop Stephen. He banged and banged until Tony finally appeared and let them in. There was someone else with him.

"Hi, guys," Tony said, before they had a chance to speak. "I'd like you to meet a very special man. This is Mr. Rooney. He donates a lot of the money that keeps the Center open, and he's the chairman of our Board of Directors.

"Mr. Rooney," he continued, "these are some of the boys I told you about. They worked hardest of all."

Mr. Rooney looked down at the boys over the top of his glasses. He reminded Stephen of his grandfather.

"Boys," he said, "you ought to be proud of yourselves. Because of your hard work, our Open House will be a success, and this Center will offer even better service to our community. Well done!"

"But the ten bucks!" Stephen burst out. "Everybody got ten bucks!"

Tony looked at the boys. Then he looked at Mr. Rooney. "If you'll excuse us, sir, the boys and I need to have a little talk."

Tony brought the boys into his office. "Listen, guys, nobody had to know what anybody else got. But, beyond that, I don't see what you have to complain about. I mean, you agreed to do a day's work for ten dollars, right?"

The boys nodded.

"And that's what I paid you, right?"

The boys nodded again.

"As far as Mark and the others go, I was desperate. I needed the help, and I knew there was no way

Mark would agree to bring his friends for less."

"But what about Sammy?" Stephen asked.

He worked hard," Tony said. "But I think you guys are missing the big picture. The Center is all painted. We're going to impress some people and hopefully stay open. And you — all of you — are responsible for that. Isn't that more important than who got paid what?"

The boys looked at each other. They still weren't sure, but they did have to agree that keeping the Center open was pretty important.

"Thanks again, guys," Tony concluded. "We couldn't have done it without you."

Stephen and his friends walked down the street, feeling happy and a little disappointed at the same time. Then Nathan said, "So what are you guys going to do with your ten dollars?"

"Comic books!" shouted Brian.

"Video games," yelled Stephen.

"Pizza!" hollered Boo. "But the last one to my house has to pay!"

Were you surprised that the boys who only painted for a few hours were paid the same amount as the boys who worked hard all day? If you answered yes, why were you surprised?

One time Jesus told his followers a story about what the kingdom of heaven will be like. Jesus' story was very much like the one you've just read. It also had a surprise ending.

Here is the story Jesus told:

Workers in a Vineyard
(Mt 20:1-16)

"Early one morning a man went out to hire some workers for his vineyard. After he had agreed to pay them the usual amount for a day's work, he sent them off to his vineyard.

"About nine that morning, the man saw some other people standing in the market with nothing to do. He said he would pay them what was fair, if they would work in his vineyard. So they went.

"At noon and again about three in the afternoon he returned to the market. And each time he made the same agreement with others who were loafing around with nothing to do.

"Finally, about five in the afternoon the man went back and found some others standing there. He asked them, 'Why have you been standing here all day long doing nothing?'

"'Because no one has hired us,' they answered. Then he told them to go work in his vineyard.

"That evening the owner of the vineyard told the man in charge of the workers to call them in and give them their money. He also told the man to begin with the ones who were hired last. When the workers arrived, the ones who had been hired at five in the afternoon were given a full day's pay.

"The workers who had been hired first thought they would be given more than the others. But when they were given the same, they began complaining to the owner of the vineyard. They said, 'The ones who were hired last worked for only one hour. But you paid them the same that you did us. And we worked in the hot sun all day long!'

"The owner answered one of them, 'Friend, I didn't cheat you. I paid you exactly what we agreed on. Take your money now and go! What business is it of yours if I want to pay them the same that I paid you? Don't I have the right to do what I want with my own money? Why should you be jealous, if I want to be generous?'"

Jesus then said, "So it is. Everyone who is now first will be last, and everyone who is last will be first."

THINK

In this story Jesus teaches us that all people have an *equal* chance to enter the kingdom of heaven. God our Father, like the vineyard owner, is very generous with his love. We should be happy, not jealous, when God is good to other people.

Have you ever felt jealous when someone else got something you wanted or you didn't think they deserved? What are some things you can do when you're tempted to feel jealous?

PRAY

Jesus, I'm glad to know that God our Father wants to welcome all people into the kingdom of heaven. Help me to live and love as you did, so that someday I'll be ready to enter this kingdom too!

A Change of Heart

Based on the Parable of the Two Sons

It's time to put out the garbage!" John's mother called. And all he could do was moan.

Monday afternoons seemed to come round lots more than once a week. And this Monday afternoon, in particular, was never supposed to be dedicated to garbage.

John's friend, Matt, had lent him a copy of *Mango Man Super 4X.* He wanted it back tomorrow. And John was just about to beat the final boss!

"Do I have to?" he shouted back, buttons and fingers flicking to the rhythm of *Mango Man's* flying fists.

"Yes, you have to," his mother answered, "or you will be spending a lot less time in front of that computer screen."

John didn't have time to argue now. He was ducking fireballs and firing at metalloid ducks. Some-how, words like "I do it every week. Can't I miss just once?" came tumbling out of his mouth.

And then — rescue.

Mango Man's partner, *Zippy-Moo,* leapt out from behind a mushroom to defeat the duck. And John's big sister, Abbey, called down from her attic room, "I'll do it, Mom. Don't worry."

Thank goodness," John's mom sighed. "At least someone in this house has a sense of responsibility. At least someone in this family appreciates that I shouldn't have to do all the chores. Thank you, Abigail. I'm off to Shop and Drop now, and I'd like the garbage out on the sidewalk before I get back."

John's mom turned one of her less-than-pleased glances toward

him, and then marched out the front door.

And that's when *Mango Man* used up his last life.

"No!" John shouted at the computer screen. "No! No! No!"

Where was the secret weapon? Where was *Zippy-Moo* when you needed him most?

What are you screaming about?" demanded Abbey. She'd wandered down from the attic and had that "you-are-so-immature" look in her eyes.

"You wouldn't understand," John snapped back. He switched off the game and flopped, sulking, on the sofa.

Abbey just shook her head and rolled her eyes.

"Well, what are you looking at, Miss Perfect-Helpful-Daughter-Who-Never-Does-Anything-Wrong?"

"Don't talk that way to me," Abbey smirked. "You're the one who got out of doing the garbage. In case you hadn't noticed, I'm actually doing you a favor!"

Abbey was right about that. Still, John couldn't help thinking that his sister's generosity had less to do with helping him out, and more to do with getting on their mom's good side.

But before he could say anything, the phone rang.

"Who? What? NO!" That's about all of the conversation that John could hear. But when Abbey hung up the phone, she seemed in an awful hurry.

"I really have to go to Jenn's house," she explained. "It's an emergency!"

"What's the matter?" John wanted to know. "What happened?"

"You wouldn't understand," was all she said. And she was out the door so fast that she never even heard John ask, "WHAT ABOUT THE GARBAGE?"

John shrugged his shoulders and shut the door. "Oh, well," he thought, "at least I have the house to myself."

The problem was, there wasn't much he wanted to do. He didn't want to go back to his game. And

there wasn't anything good on TV. So he sat on the sofa and kicked his feet. And when after about thirty seconds he got tired of that, John decided that he might just as well take out the garbage.

He ran round the house, emptying little waste baskets into a big one. Then he dumped it into one of those big black bags and tied up the top. And just as he set it on the curb in front of the house, his mother drove up.

"What are you doing?" she asked. "I thought you were too busy for that kind of work." Then she added, "Oh, I know. I bet you started to feel guilty once your sister started doing your chores."

"Nope," said John. "Abbey's not even here. She went off to visit her friend and I did the job all by myself."

John's mother gave him one of her puzzled looks. Then she disappeared into the house. And when she reappeared, there was an altogether different look on her face.

"I owe you an apology, John. Abbey is nowhere to be found. I don't know what's gotten into her."

"Well," John shrugged, "at least there's someone in this house who has a sense of responsibility. Somebody who appreciates that you shouldn't have to do all the chores."

"That was well said!" his mom replied. "And well done! But I'll tell you, that sister of yours is going to have some explaining to do when she gets home."

John just smiled.

Have you ever refused to obey your parents or teachers, like John did in the story? Did you change your mind (and heart) later and do what they had asked you to do? How did this make you feel?

Jesus once told a story about two brothers who were asked to do something by their father. One of them said no at first, but then he changed his mind and obeyed his father.

Here is Jesus' story:

A Story about Two Sons
(Mt 21:28-32)

"I will tell you a story about a man who had two sons. Then you can tell me what you think. The father went to the older son and said, 'Go work in the vineyard today!' His son told him that he would not do it, but later he changed his mind and went. The man then told his younger son to go work in the vineyard. The boy said he would, but he didn't go. Which one of the sons obeyed his father?"

"The older one," the chief priests and leaders answered.

Then Jesus told them:

"You can be sure that tax collectors and prostitutes will get into the kingdom of God before you ever will! When John the Baptist showed you how to do right, you would not believe him. But these evil people did believe. And even when you saw what they did, you still would not change your minds and believe."

In this story Jesus teaches us that what we *do* counts more than the promises we make. It's also a story about *repentance* — being sorry for acting badly.

When you've done something wrong, do you show that you're sorry by trying to do something good?

Jesus, I don't always obey my parents and teachers as you want me to. I can be like the brothers in your story. Sometimes I say no when I'm asked to do something. Sometimes I don't keep my good promises. Please let me know what's right and wrong. And help me to always do what's right.

Just in Time

Based on the Parable of the Ten Bridesmaids

It was a warm afternoon for November. And it was a good thing, because Ashley and Lee Ann and the rest of their classmates had been standing at the corner for half an hour.

"We'll miss the hayride!" Ashley moaned. "I just know it!"

"No, we won't," Lee Ann assured her friend. "If the whole bus is late, they'll have to wait for us."

"What do you think happened?" Ashley wondered.

"I don't know," said Lee Ann. "Maybe the bus broke down. Or maybe they had to stop because the Johnson twins were throwing stuff out the back window again. I hope there wasn't an accident."

Just then Lee Ann's mom came running up the street.

"Listen, everybody," she announced. "The school just called. The bus had a flat tire, so they're sending another one. They said you should stay here and wait. The new bus will be along any time now."

"This will take forever!" Ashley moaned again. "And I was really looking forward to this hayride."

"Me, too," sighed Lee Ann, slipping off her knapsack. "I brought loads of great snacks to eat!"

Snacks?" said Ashley. "I didn't bring any snacks. I thought we'd have something at the hayride."

"No," explained Lee Ann. "Didn't you read the paper they sent home? We were supposed to bring our own food."

"Well, I'd better run up to the Mini-Mart and buy some, then."

"There isn't time!" Lee Ann shouted. "The bus could be here any minute. Why don't you just share mine?"

"Because your mom always buys those icky, crunchy, cheesy things," Ashley said, making a face. "I'll be right back."

Ashley hurried off. All Lee Ann could do was hope that the bus wouldn't come.

Five minutes later, Ashley was back. There was still no sign of the bus.

"See?" Ashley smiled knowingly. "I told you. It'll be ages before that bus gets here!"

"Well, I'm going to have a drink, then," said Lee Ann, twisting the lid off her plastic thermos.

"Drinks!" shouted Ashley. "We have to bring our own drinks, too?"

"That's what the paper said," Lee Ann sighed. "Here, you can have some of mine."

"No thanks," snorted Ashley, sniffing the contents of the thermos.

"It's just hot chocolate," said Lee Ann.

"With marshmallows! I happen to hate marshmallows!" Ashley exclaimed. "Looks like I need to go back to the Mini-Mart." And off she ran.

"Wait!" Lee Ann shouted. "What about the bus?"

But Ashley kept on running. She bought two root beers and a couple of candy bars, then walked back to the bus stop.

"I was worried the whole time you were gone," Lee Ann said. "What if the bus had come?"

"It didn't, did it?" Ashley smiled. "So there's no problem, right?"

"I guess not," Lee Ann sighed, pulling on her mittens. "It's getting cold, isn't it?"

"Yeah," Ashley shivered. "I sure wish I'd brought my gloves."

"Here, have one of mine," Lee Ann offered. "I'll keep one hand in my pocket."

"No, yours are too small," said Ashley. "You know what? I think I have time to run home and get a pair of my own."

"No way!" said Lee Ann, shaking her head.

"Yes way!" Ashley shouted, as she bounded down the street.

"The bus! What about the bus?" Lee Ann called. But Ashley kept on running. And as soon as she turned

the corner at the bottom of the street...the bus arrived!

What could Lee Ann do? She thought about attempting to run after her friend, but she'd never get back before the bus was loaded. So she went to the back of the line to make sure she was the last to board.

"Come on," the driver called to her. "We're late!"

"But my friend is on her way," Lee Ann explained. "She'll be here any minute. Can't we just wait a little longer?"

"Sorry, kid," the driver said. "Your friend had plenty of time to get here. It's not my fault she's going to miss the bus. Or yours either. If she wanted to go to the hayride, it was up to her to be ready."

Reluctantly, Lee Ann climbed into the bus. The door shut behind her. Lee Ann sighed. Ashley was sure disorganized, but the hayride just wouldn't be the same without her.

The bus finally pulled into the parking area. Its doors creaked open and all the kids piled out. Lee Ann linked up with some other girls and crawled onto a prickly hay mound. Right as the hayride was about to begin, a car horn blew loudly. Lee Ann heard a familiar voice cry, "Wait for me!"

"Over here, Ashley!" Lee Ann yelled. "There's still room!"

Ashley scrambled onto the wagon. "Thanks again, Mom!" she shouted with a wave. "I'll be *sure* to catch the bus home!"

Have you ever been left behind or left out of something because you weren't ready when everyone else was? How did that make you feel?

In St. Matthew's Gospel we find a story Jesus once told about being ready.

Here is Jesus' story:

A Story about Ten Girls
(Mt 25:1–13)

"The kingdom of heaven is like what happened one night when ten girls took their oil lamps and went to a wedding to meet the groom. Five of the girls were foolish and five were wise. The foolish ones took their lamps, but no extra oil. The ones who were wise took along extra oil for their lamps.

"The groom was late arriving, and the girls became drowsy and fell asleep. Then in the middle of the night someone shouted, 'Here's the groom! Come to meet him!'

"When the girls got up and started getting their lamps ready, the foolish ones said to the others, 'Let us have some of your oil! Our lamps are going out.'

"The girls who were wise answered, 'There's not enough oil for all of us! Go and buy some for yourselves.' While the foolish girls were on their way to get some oil, the groom arrived. The girls who were ready went in to the wedding, and the doors were closed. Later the other girls returned and shouted, 'Sir, sir! Open the door for us!'

"But the groom replied, 'I don't even know you!'

"So, my disciples, always be ready! You don't know the day or the time when all this will happen."

In this story Jesus is telling us that we should always be ready for the time when he will come again at the end of our lives or the end of the world. We want to prepare for Jesus' coming by living just as he taught us.

THINK

What are some ways you can keep ready and waiting for Jesus?

PRAY

Jesus, my parents and teachers have taught me how you want me to live. Now help me to do it! Then I'll always be ready to greet you when you come.

Anderson's Wait

Based on the Parable of the Seed Growing by Itself

On the first day of the first week in September, Anderson ate the first apple from his family's apple tree. But after the first bite, Anderson noticed that something was wrong. With the tip of his tongue, Anderson pushed at the back of his top left front tooth.

It moved.

Anderson ran to his room and looked in the mirror above his dresser. He pushed the tooth again, and could see it barely wiggle.

Arturo, the stuffed pterodactyl, peered over Anderson's shoulder. "Oh, dear!" he cried. "The boy's tooth is loose!"

"No problem, man," shouted Hans, the toy foreman who drove the toy bulldozer. "I'll get my crew up there with some concrete. We'll have it solid again in no time."

"No," said Anderson quickly. "It's a baby tooth. It's supposed to come out."

"Oh, dear!" Arturo shuddered. "The boy's tooth has got to come out!"

"No problem, man," shouted Hans. "I'll get my crew up there with some shovels. We'll have it out in no time."

Arturo wrapped his wings around his face. "Oh, dear! Oh, dear!" he cried.

"Dynamite!" shouted Hans. "We'll use dynamite! Quick and easy."

And that's when someone tapped on Anderson's window. Anderson opened it, and there was Granny, the Apple Tree.

"I couldn't help overhearing you boys," she chuckled. "And I have

only one thing to say:

*As surely as babies grow and are
    born,*
As surely as seedlings sprout,
*All that God plans comes to pass in
    its time,*
And Anderson's tooth will fall out!"

Then, shutting the window with one of her branches, she whispered, "All you have to do is wait."

"That sounds good to me," said Anderson. And he went downstairs for supper.

On the second day of the second week of September, Anderson was just finishing his second plate of spaghetti, when his wiggly tooth hit a meatball. Anderson ran into his room and looked in the mirror. His wiggly tooth was now wobbly.

"Oh, dear!" cried Arturo. "The boy's tooth is moving again."

"It won't be long," whispered Pig the Bank.

"Long 'til what?" asked Anderson.

"Until we're all rich!" grinned Pig.

"Money?" shrieked Arturo, falling to the floor. "Is that all you can

think about at a time like this? Money? The boy's tooth is falling out!"

"Yes," said Pig, rubbing his trotters together. "And when it has fallen out, the tooth fairies will come and give us GOLD for it!"

"A quarter," said Anderson. "My mom said a quarter."

"No problem, man," shouted Hans. "I'll get my crew up there with a tractor and some good strong rope. We'll have it out in no time."

"Let's do it now!" Pig squealed with excitement. "We can be rich by morning."

Anderson clasped his hands over his mouth. And a brown branch with gold-edged leaves brushed against his window.

"I believe you boys have forgotten what I said," Granny the Apple Tree gently scolded. "So let me remind you:

*As surely as leaves drop to earth in
    the fall,*
As surely as geese fly south,
*All that God plans comes to pass in
    its time,*

And Anderson's tooth will fall out!

"So be patient," she concluded. "And leave the boy alone!"

On the third day of the third week of September, Anderson was finishing his third bowl of pudding. He was trying to be careful. But wobble met wobble, and *whack* — Anderson's tooth was downright wonky.

Anderson ran to his room and looked in the mirror. He could now push his tooth so far forward that it stuck straight out.

"Oh, dear!" howled a hovering Arturo. "The boy's tooth will never be the same again. I can't bear to see it move like that."

"Nonsense!" called Dr. Webb the spider from her home high in the corner, where the walls met the ceiling. "There is nothing to be afraid of. This is very interesting." And she swung down onto Anderson's face to have a closer look.

"Don't hurt the boy!" begged Arturo.

"Doctors cost money," grunted Pig the Bank.

Anderson said nothing.

Dr. Webb pushed the tooth backward. She pulled it forward. Then, finally she pushed it back again to where it should have been.

"Just like a gate," she scribbled in her notebook. Then she pulled out her magnifying glass and carefully inspected the tooth.

"It should come out any day now," she concluded.

"Any day now. Hmmm." Pig was punching numbers into his calculator.

"I'll have it out sooner than that!" Hans was loading a jackhammer into the back of a toy truck.

"Enough! Enough!" Arturo was rolling around on the floor.

"I could schedule you for surgery in the next ten minutes or so," Dr. Webb said, checking her instruments.

And then the window blew open and a bunch of brown leaves blew in.

"I'll say this just once more," called Granny the Apple Tree.

"As surely as caterpillars burst their cocoons
And butterflies flutter about,
All that God plans comes to pass in its time,
And Anderson's tooth will fall out!

"It's just about ready," she said. "Why not wait?"

On the very next day,
as Arturo nervously nibbled on his claws,
as Hans demolished a building-block bridge,
as Pig tried to pull the cork out of his nose,
as the Doctor operated on a careless fly,
Anderson's tooth finally fell out.

He was just sitting on his bed, reading. He closed his mouth, and when he opened it again, the tooth was gone.

"Gone!" wailed Arturo. "The boy's tooth is gone!"

"Gone?" Pig complained. "It had better not be gone. The tooth fairies are very particular. You have to produce a tooth to get the loot."

"Gone," noted the Doctor in her records.

"Gone," sighed Hans, as he put away his wrecking ball.

Gone," said Granny, as her bare branches brushed against the window. "Gone, like my beautiful leaves. But not for long. Listen:

As surely as leaves start from stems in the spring,

And eggs shake and quiver and crack,
All that God plans comes to pass in its time,
And Anderson's tooth will come back!"

Anderson looked at his friends and smiled a missing-tooth smile. Then he picked up his tooth from where it had fallen, and took it to show his mom.

In this story Anderson's toys come to life. They are impatient for his tooth to fall out. But the wise Apple Tree reminds them that God has a plan for Anderson. She explains that Anderson's tooth will fall out according to this plan.

Here's something wonderful to think about: God has a special plan for you! Even though you can't see him, God is always at work in your life.

One time, Jesus told a story about God's plan to make his kingdom grow.

This is the story:

Another Story about Seeds
(Mk 4:26-29)

LISTEN

"God's kingdom is like what happens when a farmer scatters seed in a field. The farmer sleeps at night and is up and around during the day. Yet the seeds keep sprouting and growing, and he doesn't understand how. It is the ground that makes the seeds sprout and grow into plants that produce grain. Then when harvest season comes and the grain is ripe, the farmer cuts it with a sickle."

The seeds the farmer plants in this story are like the teachings of Jesus. In God's plan Jesus began the kingdom of God here on earth. In God's plan Jesus' teachings keep on spreading, and God's kingdom keeps on quietly growing.

THINK

What can you do today to help the kingdom of God grow here on earth?

PRAY

Jesus, I'm happy to belong to your kingdom, the kingdom of God. I know that just like the seeds in your story, this kingdom is growing bigger and stronger day by day. I want to help it grow by all that I think, say and do.

The Contest

Based on the Parable of the Mustard Seed

Big Brown Bear stood on top of the mountain. The mountain on top of the world. He looked at the hills and the rivers and the forests below. Then he threw back his huge head and shouted: "I am Big Brown Bear. I stand on the mountain on top of the world. No one is stronger than I!"

Just at that moment, Bighorn Sheep climbed to the top of the mountain. The mountain on top of the world. He saw Big Brown Bear. He heard him boast and brag. So he rammed his horned head hard against a tree — CRACK! — and followed it with his reply. "I am Bighorn Sheep. I stand on the mountain on top of the world. No one is stronger than I!"

Then a voice shrieked from the sky. "I am Big Bald Eagle. I soar above the mountain. I am master of earth and air. No one is stronger than I!"

"Don't be silly!" peeped a small voice. "I am the strongest creature on this or any mountain."

Big Brown Bear looked.
Bighorn Sheep looked.
Big Bald Eagle looked.

Then Little Gray Squirrel popped out from behind a boulder, with her two children chattering and chuckling after her.

"You tell 'em, Mama," said the first one.

"You're the strongest of them all," said the second.

Big Bald Eagle snickered.
Bighorn Sheep snorted.
Big Brown Bear howled.
Little Gray Squirrel stood up straight. She crossed her arms and flicked her bushy tail. "Let's have

a contest, then," she said, "and we shall see who is strongest."

But the bear, the sheep, and the eagle only laughed.

Little Gray Squirrel watched them for a minute, then she shrugged and turned. "Come along, children," she called. "They don't believe they can win. Otherwise they would have accepted my challenge."

"I bet they're scared," chattered one of the children.

"Chicken-lickens," chortled the other.

And with that, the laughing stopped.

"Me? Scared?" snarled Big Brown Bear. "Never!"

"I'm not afraid of anything!" Bighorn Sheep declared.

"Particularly some snack-size squirrel," shrieked Big Bald Eagle.

"We accept your challenge!" they shouted together.

"Very well, then," Little Gray Squirrel nodded. "In seven sunrises we will meet again at this very spot. The mountain on top of the world."

When the day came, nearly every animal in the forest had heard of the contest. Raccoons and rabbits. Muskrats and moose. Cougars and caribou, too. They all gathered on the mountain. The mountain on top of the world.

Then Big Brown Bear arrived, growling and shaking his shaggy head.

Bighorn Sheep followed, shoving and snorting his way through the crowd.

Finally, Big Bald Eagle dropped from the sky, his mighty wingspan blocking the sun. He cocked his head and peered at the animals. "I see Big Brown Bear," he sneered. "I see Bighorn Sheep. I see many different creatures. But I do not see the one who called us here. Is it possible that Little Gray Squirrel is not as brave and strong as she thinks?"

"Oh, no," came a voice from behind the boulder. "But I am late, and I apologize. I had a rather important errand to run."

"Very important," chuckled one of her children.

"Absolutely essential," chortled the other.

"All right, then," roared the bear. "Let's get on with it. Are we going to wrestle or fight or what?"

"Oh, no," said Little Gray Squirrel again, appearing now on top of the huge boulder. She crossed her arms and flicked her bushy tail. "Do you see this boulder I'm sitting on?"

They nodded.

"We're going to see who can move it."

Move it? thought Big Brown Bear. *But it's taller than I am!*

Move it? thought Bighorn Sheep. *It has to weigh a hundred times more than I do!*

Move it? thought Big Bald Eagle. *I can't even get my claws around it!*

But none of them said what he thought. They just grunted and growled, stamped and shrieked, confident that none of them would be able to move the enormous boulder from its perch on the mountain. The mountain on top of the world. They would have to move on to something smaller.

Big Brown Bear went first. He stood on his back legs. He spread his furry arms wide. And he wrapped them, as best he could, around the boulder. Then he groaned, he grunted, he growled. He roared, he strained, he shook! But the boulder did not move.

Bighorn Sheep went next. He stared at the boulder for a moment, then he stepped slowly backward, almost to the edge of the mountain. He breathed in deeply. He pawed at the ground. Then he lowered his head and ran straight for the boulder as fast as he could. CRACK! crashed his horns against the rock. And the sound boomed and echoed across the valleys. But the boulder did not move.

As Bighorn Sheep staggered dizzily away, Big Bald Eagle took to the sky. He disappeared into a cloud and then appeared again, flying straight for the sun. He wheeled and turned and with a scream headed for the boulder — which looked like only a speck, far below. But as he got closer, the boulder looked bigger. Bigger and wider and heavier! And just when it looked like he would crash right into it, he screamed again and turned away.

This is foolish!" he cried. "Risking our lives to move something no one could possibly budge!"

"I haven't had my turn yet," Little Gray Squirrel said.

"That's right," said one of her children.

"Fair's fair," said the other.

Big Brown Bear looked at the mother squirrel. "If the three of us couldn't move it, how could you even hope to?"

Little Gray Squirrel said nothing. She just skittered off of the boulder to the ground below. Her children followed close behind.

"How about here, Mama?" asked one of the young squirrels.

"Or over here?" suggested the other.

Little Gray Squirrel chose a spot halfway between the two, just outside the shadow of the boulder. Then she dug up the ground and dropped a tiny seed into the hole. As her children covered the seed with dirt, she turned to the others and said: "There. I've done it."

"Done what?" asked Bighorn Sheep.

"Everything I need to do to move the boulder. Now all we have to do is wait."

"Nobody said anything about waiting!" moaned Big Bald Eagle. "You have to move it NOW!"

"I don't remember that rule," said Little Gray Squirrel.

"Neither do we," chimed in the two little squirrels.

And so they waited. For an hour. For a day. For three days. For a week. One by one, the other animals left, until only the competitors remained.

"I'm leaving," said Big Bald Eagle at last.

"Me, too," said Bighorn Sheep.

"I still say we should have wrestled," grumbled Big Brown Bear.

"Look!" shouted Little Gray Squirrel.

"We knew it would happen!" shouted one of her children.

"All we had to do was wait!" shouted the other.

Something small and green and tender was pushing its way out of the ground.

"All right," agreed the eagle. "Something has happened here. So we shall keep coming back. And we shall watch. And we shall see if the boulder moves."

And the animals did come back. They and their children and their children's children. A squirrel's lifetime passed. And a sheep's. And an eagle's. And a bear's. The story passed from generation to generation. And the acorn the squirrel planted grew into a tree.

The bears would come in the summers to rub their shaggy backs against it. The sheep would come in winters to chew off bits of bark. The eagles would come in spring to nest and raise their young. And the squirrels built their home in the trunk so that they might keep watch all year round.

The roots of that great oak reached under the huge boulder. The roots stretched and swelled and grew. Finally, many years later, it happened. With a thunderous sound, the boulder tumbled down the mountain!

A Little Gray Squirrel and a tiny seed had accomplished what even the strongest beasts could not do. At the mountain on top of the world, the contest was finished…at last.

Did the ending of this story surprise you? If it did, why were you surprised?

The story shows us that great and wonderful things can sometimes start out very small and hidden. Jesus used a story something like this one to teach his followers about God's kingdom.

This is the story Jesus told:

A Mustard Seed
(Mk 4:30–32)

LISTEN

"What is God's kingdom like? What story can I use to explain it? It is like what happens when a mustard seed is planted in the ground. It is the smallest seed in all the world. But once it is planted, it grows larger than any garden plant. It even puts out branches that are big enough for birds to nest in its shade."

THINK

The kingdom of God is already here with us. Not everyone knows about it yet. But God is making it grow and spread, just like the tiny mustard seed that grew into the biggest of all the plants.

Can you think of some new and speedy ways to let people know about God's kingdom and how they can belong to it?

PRAY

Jesus, thank you for coming to earth to tell us about God's kingdom. I want everyone in the world to know about it and to belong to it!

Camel and the Needle's Eye

Based on the Parable of the Camel and the Eye of the Needle

Camel was proud of his neck. It was long and straight — the perfect perch for his wide, handsome head.

Camel was proud of his legs, too. They were tall and strong, and could carry him through the deepest sand dunes.

But most of all, Camel was proud of his hump. It was much more impressive than the hairy lump most camels carried around on their backs. This was a mighty mountain of a hump that could store a week's worth of water, or more!

Camel had a master. A master who was proud, as well. He was proud of his bags of gold. He was proud of his sacks of silver. He was proud of his jewelry and his fine clothes, and of the twenty body-

guards he needed to protect him everywhere he went.

Camel's master was a merchant. He bought in one town. He sold in another. And he never failed to add to his fortune.

Between the towns, however, lay the desert. It was vast, silent and very unpredictable. Its weather could change at any minute. And that's just what happened this one day....

First there was a breeze. Camel sucked the hot breath into his flat, floppy nose. Then the breeze whipped into a wind. It picked up sand and sent it stinging through the caravan. Camel shut his eyes. The merchant wrapped his robe around his face. Finally, the wind howled itself into a storm. Camel and the merchant could neither hear nor

see. They wandered blindly, this way and that, hoping the bodyguards were near. But when the storm at last ended, Camel and the merchant were alone.

"No need to worry," snorted Camel. "My long neck, my tall legs, and my mighty hump will get us safely to the town."

"Indeed," echoed the merchant, shaking sand out of his robes. "My bodyguards will find us. That's what I pay them for."

But the bodyguards had gotten lost themselves. And Camel and the merchant were unable to find the town. The storm had changed the face of the desert. They were completely lost!

They wandered for one day, for two days, for three, growing ever more thirsty and hungry and hot. And then, on the fourth day, they saw it — on oasis, rising tall and green against the dusty horizon!

Camel was glad he had such a long neck and tall legs. He raced for the oasis, with the merchant slumped in a heap on his hump. But just as Camel was about to step into the cool oasis, a huge lion sprang up out of the desert, blocking his way.

"Welcome!" the lion roared. It was a friendly roar, but the lion did not step aside.

Move away, you beast!" shouted the merchant. And he pulled out a bright sharp sword with a jeweled handle.

"Such things will not be necessary here," the lion roared back. And the breath of that roar rushed out like the wind and turned the sword to dust!

"This is a very special place," the lion continued. "And you are both welcome to enter, to take freely whatever you want, and to stay as long as you like."

"We ask for no charity," the merchant answered. "We have gold and silver enough to buy this puny place and twenty more like it."

"Perhaps," the lion grinned. "Assuming, of course, that you can get in."

"Get in?" huffed the merchant, growing more impatient and even thirstier. "Why, the way is clear — once you move aside."

"But you haven't yet seen the gate," the lion replied. Then he bent his head toward a tiny shiny thing stuck in the sand, right in front of Camel and the merchant.

"What's that?" the merchant demanded.

It's a needle," the lion answered. "And the eye of the needle is the gate to this oasis."

"The gate?" the merchant shouted. "That's ridiculous! No one could squeeze through a gate that small."

"If you are not interested in going through, perhaps your camel, here, would like to try."

The merchant threw his hands into the air. "Again I say, *ridiculous!* This is the largest camel in the kingdom. This is the finest camel that money can buy. There is no way that this camel will fit through the eye of that needle. But if he would like to try," the merchant concluded, "he is more than welcome."

And then the merchant gathered up his bags of gold and silver and jewels, strapped them safely to his own back, and leaped down into the sand.

Camel looked at his master. He looked at the lion. He looked at the pool of water sitting in the middle of the oasis. Then he ran a long dry tongue across his lips.

"Yes," he said slowly. "I would like to try."

"Very good," the lion purred. "But you will need some help."

"Well, I'm not pushing him through," scoffed the merchant.

"No," continued the lion. "What I mean, Camel, is...well...your neck for example. You don't need a long neck in this garden. Everything is well within reach. Could we shorten it a bit?"

Camel thought for a minute. He had always been proud of that neck. But he was awfully thirsty. Slowly, he nodded "yes."

The lion went on. "And then there are those legs. Tall and knobby. Much too difficult to work through the gate. But this garden is so small, you won't really need them here. Shall we shorten the legs, too?"

This was harder for Camel. But, oh, the shade and the water looked so good! So again he nodded.

"And finally..." concluded the lion.

Camel swallowed hard. He could guess what was coming.

"Finally, there is the matter of that hump. Very useful for storing water in the desert, I will agree. But storing and hoarding are not necessary in the garden. Everything is free. And besides, that hump will never fit through the gate."

Impossible, thought Camel. His hump was his pride and joy. How could he let it go? And yet, it was clearly doing him no good at the moment. It was hard, very hard, but, finally, he decided.

"I will leave my hump," he announced, "and go through the gate."

The lion grinned and gave a mighty roar. The wind answered his call and whipped up around Camel until he disappeared in a whirling funnel of sand. Then the funnel swirled through the eye of the needle, like one half of an hourglass emptying into another. It settled finally in the shade of a palm tree, and when it had spun itself out, there was Camel again. At least the merchant assumed it was Camel. Short, light, and graceful, he looked very different from the beast that had carried the merchant across the desert.

"Well," the merchant laughed. "I don't mind a few little changes. Surely it's better than starving. And I always thought my nose was too long, anyway. Go ahead," he said to the lion. "Take a few inches off my waist, while you're at it. Pull me through the needle, too."

The lion did not laugh back. Instead, he looked very serious.

"I don't think you understand," he answered. "To get through the needle, your camel had to be willing to lose what he was proud of. He had to trust me, and me alone, to get him through.

"With him that meant losing some leg and neck and hump. But with you that means losing a far different kind of weight. Those sacks tied on your back, for instance. The gold around your neck. The jewels, the rings, the silver. There is no need for such things in my garden. Everything is free. Your treasures will never pass through the gate."

The merchant just stared at the lion. Then he shouted, "Give up my silver? Give up my gold? Just to get into your stupid oasis? Impossible!"

"But you saw your camel," the lion reminded him. "If he could get through, nothing is impossible for you."

Legs and humps are different," muttered the merchant. "It's harder for me, that's all." Then he turned away from the oasis, made sure the gold was tied securely to his back, and trudged off into the desert.

He walked a hundred yards, then turned around for one last look. But by then, Camel had joined the other animals in the pool, the lion had sunk down again into the sand, and the whole oasis was already shaking in the hot light — until, finally, it shimmered itself away.

"Impossible!" said the merchant one last time. Then he shook his head and wandered off, his wealth piled up like a hump on his back.

In this story, Camel had to give up something he really liked in order to get something even better. Have you ever had to give up something in order to get something better? What did you give up? What did you get in return?

One time, a rich man asked Jesus what he had to do to have eternal life. Jesus told him that he had to keep all of the commandments. Jesus also told the man that he should sell everything he owned, give the money to the poor and then come and follow him. The rich man went away very sad. He didn't want to give up all the nice things he had — not even to gain eternal life! Jesus looked around at his disciples.

Then he told them a little story:

A Rich Man
(Mk 10:23-31)

LISTEN

"It's hard for rich people to get into God's kingdom!" The disciples were shocked to hear this. So Jesus told them again, "It's terribly hard to get into God's kingdom! In fact, it's easier for a camel to go through the eye of a needle than for a rich person to get into God's kingdom."

Jesus' disciples were even more amazed. They asked each other, "How can anyone ever be saved?"

Jesus looked at them and said, "There are some things that people cannot do, but God can do anything."

Peter replied, "Remember, we left everything to be your followers!"

Jesus told him:

"You can be sure that anyone who gives up home or brothers or sisters or mother or father or children or land for me and for the Good News will be rewarded. In this world they will be given a hundred times as many houses and brothers and sisters and mothers and children and pieces of land, though they will also be mistreated. And in the world to come, they will have eternal life. But many who are now first will be last, and many who are now last will be first."

THINK

Jesus teaches us that money and things can keep us away from God's kingdom if we make them too important. Jesus wants us to give *God* the first place in our heart. God and the eternal life he promises us are greater and more important than all the money or things in the world!

What things are especially important to you? Don't let them become more important than God or the special people in your life.

PRAY

Jesus, I want God to be first in my life. Help me never to let anything else become more important to me. I believe that you are God's Son and that you will give me eternal life.

Ready or Not

Based on the Parable of the Master's Unexpected Return

Mrs. Finkle is coming over this afternoon, Anderson. She and I have some grown-up things to discuss. And while she is here, I expect you to tidy up this room of yours."

"Aw, Mom," moaned Anderson. "Do I have to? I cleaned it up two days ago."

"And you've managed to make it twice as messy in between. I want it clean by the time Mrs. Finkle leaves. I'll come up to check, and if it's not spotless, you can forget about going to the ball game tonight. I mean it," she added and the door closed behind her with a click.

"She looks serious," whispered Arturo, the stuffed pterodactyl. "We'd better do it right away."

"My men and I will give you a hand," shouted Hans, the toy foreman, from the floor. "My bulldozer is ready to go."

"Then let's get started," Anderson sighed.

"Wait a minute. What's the hurry?" came a sleepy voice from Anderson's bed. It was Catnap, the pillowcase. "When Mrs. Finkle comes," he yawned, "she talks for hours and hours and hours. Play awhile. Rest awhile. You can always clean up later. You have all the time in the world!"

Anderson stopped and thought. "You're right about Mrs. Finkle," he agreed. Then he smiled. "Okay, let's play!"

"But what if she doesn't stay so long?" whimpered a worried

Arturo. "What if she has to leave early and go to the grocery store or pick up her kids? We don't know, do we?"

"All right," Anderson decided. "How about if you keep a lookout for us. Watch through the keyhole, and if you see my mom coming, let us know."

So while Arturo hovered in front of the keyhole, Anderson played. He got out his dinosaur collection. He got out his racetrack. He pieced together half a puzzle.

And it wasn't long before his room was even messier than when he'd started!

"Ding-dong. Tick-tock," announced Robert the Radio Rabbit. His ears were antennae. His nose was a control knob. And in the middle of his belly an alarm clock ticked away.

"Two hours have passed," he chimed. "Maybe you ought to clean up."

"I'm ready when you are," called Hans, his crane poised over the toy box.

"N-no one in sight," stuttered Arturo. "But you never know. Your mom could be here any time now."

But Catnap just stretched and rolled over. "Plenty of time left," he grunted. "Play on."

Anderson grinned. The others just sighed.

Anderson took out his Junior Scientist Set this time. And his Robot Raiders. And the pieces from three different model kits.

"Ding-dong. Tick-tock," warned Robert the Radio Rabbit. "Another hour's passed. And you've got so many toys out now that I can't even see the floor!"

"My men! I've lost my men!" shouted Hans.

"Would you all please be quiet?" purred Catnap. "I'm trying to get some sleep."

And that's when Arturo yelled, "AAAAGH! She's coming! Your mom's coming! I can hear her on the stairs!" And off he flew in wild panicky circles round and round the room.

"Calm down!" shouted Anderson. "We have to hurry. And we have to work together."

"I'm too nervous!" shrieked Arturo.

"I'm too tired," yawned Catnap.

"I still can't find my men!" hollered Hans.

So Anderson had to clean up all by himself. He turned up Robert's radio as loud as he could just to cover the noise. Then he pushed toys under his bed, into his closet, behind his dresser — and into every other hiding place he could find.

"Ding-dong. Tick-tock," chimed Robert. "It's been five minutes. How long do you think it takes your mother to walk up the stairs?"

"Not that long," said Anderson. He turned Robert down, put an ear to the door, and listened. Someone was humming in the room across the hall. Anderson bent down and put his eye to the keyhole. Mrs. Finkle was just coming out of the den!

"You silly bird," he said to Arturo. "That's not my mom at all."

"Looks like you did all that work for nothing," mewed Catnap.

"I just wanted to be careful," apologized Arturo.

"I found my men!" shouted Hans. "What can we do for you here?"

"Nothing," sighed Anderson. "It's all cleaned up."

"It certainly is!" said Anderson's mom as she burst into the room.

Anderson jumped. Everyone else went still.

"Mrs. Finkle told me there was an awful commotion coming from your room. She said you must have been working very hard. And she was right! I don't think I've ever seen your room this neat."

Anderson sighed in relief and just smiled. Catnap gave him a knowing wink. What luck!

And then Anderson's mom spotted the trader's card on the floor. Near the corner of his bed.

"You just missed one little thing," she smiled cheerfully. But when she bent over to pick it up, she happened to glance under the bed.

"Anderson..." she said, a little less cheerfully. "What's this?"

"Ummm...well..." stammered Anderson.

"Don't toys belong in the toy box, or neatly stacked in the closet?"

She opened the closet door. "Anderson!" she said again, a lot less cheerfully this time. "This closet is a mess!" And it wasn't long before she discovered the mess behind his dresser, and the mess behind his bookcase, and the messes that he'd shoved into all his favorite hiding places.

"Anderson!" she called one last time. And there wasn't even a hint of cheerfulness in her voice. "There won't be any ballgame for you tonight. You're going to clean this room!"

Later that night, as Anderson was nearly finished with his room, he switched on Robert the Radio Rabbit. "Ding-dong. Tick-tock. The count is two and two, and the bases are loaded in the bottom of the ninth," Robert reported.

"You don't have to rub it in," Anderson moaned.

"But your room is really clean, this time," ticked Robert. "And it only took you five hours!"

"My men are ready for a rest," said Hans.

"My wings are tired," puffed Arturo.

"What's the hurry?" called Catnap. "Your mother won't check until morning. We have all night to finish."

"No, we don't," said Anderson. "And besides, I only have one job left." Then he looked at the others and grinned. "It's time to change my pillowcase!"

In this fantasy story Anderson put off cleaning his room until the very last minute. He wasn't really ready when his mom came to check it out.

Has anything like that ever happened to you? How did it feel not to be ready?

Jesus has left us a short story about being ready for the day when he will come back to judge the world. Even though we don't know when this is going to happen, we always need to be ready and waiting.

Here is Jesus' story:

No One Knows the Day or Time
(Mk 13:32–37)

"No one knows the day or the time [when Jesus will come to judge the world]. The angels in heaven don't know, and the Son himself doesn't know. Only the Father knows. So watch out and be ready! You don't know when the time will come. It is like what happens when a man goes away for a while and places his servants in charge of everything. He tells each of them what to do, and he orders the guard to keep alert. So be alert! You don't know when the master of the house will come back. It could be in the evening or at midnight or before dawn or in the morning.

"But if he comes suddenly, don't let him find you asleep. I tell everyone just what I have told you. Be alert!"

In this story, the master of the house stands for Jesus, and the servants stand for each one of us. Jesus asks us to pay attention and to be ready to meet him when he comes again.

We know that Jesus will return in glory at the end of the world. But in the meantime, he continues to come to us in different ways. We just have to be alert enough to recognize him.

One special way that Jesus comes to us is through the sacraments and prayer. We receive Jesus into our hearts whenever we receive the Holy Eucharist at Mass.

In what others ways does Jesus come to you?

PRAY

Jesus, help me to recognize the different ways you come to me each day. Sometimes you come through other people. Sometimes you come through the words of the Gospel. Sometimes you even come to me through a beautiful sunset that reminds me of how good and great you are. Keep me awake and alert. I don't ever want to miss you when you come!

Not Now, Chuckiebee!

Based on the Parable of the Persistent Friend

It was one o'clock, Saturday morning. Jennifer Ross was almost asleep. It had been a long drive, but she and her parents had finally arrived at Aunt Sue's. The plan was to spend the whole Christmas holiday there, cross-country skiing through the woods behind her aunt's cozy farmhouse.

Jennie was excited. So excited, in fact, that she was only now falling asleep. Driving...skiing...Christmas...the scenes followed one another in her head, moving more and more slowly, until...

"JENNIE! COUSIN JENNIE! WANNAPLAY!?"

Jennie opened her eyes and turned her head. Not two inches from her face were the bright eyes and toothless grin of Chuckiebee.

"WANNAPLAY?" he shouted again. "PLEEEEEEASE!"

Chuckiebee was only two, and his real name was actually Charles. But everyone called him Chuckiebee, because he never stopped buzzing around like a bee.

"Hello, Chuckiebee," Jennie yawned. "It's still the middle of the night. You'd better go back to bed."

"Don't wanna go back to bed. Wanna play! PLEEEEASE!"

Look," said Jennie, "how about if you crawl into bed with me? Then we can both get some sleep."

Chuckiebee frowned at Jennie. And then, just as she thought he was going to start shouting again, his eyes opened wide, and he said, "Okay. Be back." Jennie rolled over. She shut her eyes. And as soon as she fell back to sleep, something came crashing down on her head.

"PIGGY! HORSIE! TEDDY!"

Jennie sighed and blinked. It was raining stuffed cats and dogs — and a zoofull of other animals.

"Chuckiebee, what are you doing?" she moaned.

"WANNAPLAY? PLEEEEEE-EASE!"

"No, I told you I don't want to play. It's late. I'm really tired. But you can stay here if you'll be quiet and go to sleep."

Chuckie stopped. He dropped his last piece of ammunition. Then he crawled up onto the bed, through the jungle of stuffed animals, and curled up beside Jennie.

"Okay," he said. "Night, night."

Jennie rolled over. "Finally," she whispered to herself. And she was off.

Jennie started to dream. She was in the woods. She spotted a rabbit. She spotted a groundhog. She spotted a deer. But when they spotted her, they didn't run away. They moved towards her, slowly at first, and then more and more quickly! Other animals joined them, and soon there were hun-dreds of them chasing after her. Branches bent, leaves tumbled, and the forest shook as Jennie tried to get away. But the animals were too fast for her, and soon they had caught up to her and knocked her to the ground. They were running over her now, pads and paws and hooves pounding on her back... "WANNAPLAY! WANNAPLAY!" Suddenly Jennie realized that the little feet running up and down on her back belonged not to bunnies or beavers or even to woodchucks, but to Chuckiebee. "Stop kicking me!" she grunted.

"WANNAPLAY!" he repeated.

"That's it!" she growled, as she picked up her little cousin and carried him to his room.

"NO!" hollered Chuckiebee.

"Be quiet," Jennie demanded. "Or you'll wake everybody else up, too."

But Chuckie kicked and wriggled. He didn't stop, even when Jennie finally plunked him down on his own bed.

"Now go to sleep!" pleaded Jennie.

"WANNAPLAY! Wannaplay!" he pleaded back. He was quieter, now, and his little bottom lip was starting to shake.

"All right. All right," said Jennie. "How about this? We'll both go back to sleep right now, but first thing in the morning, I'll play with you for as long as you want."

"Really?" asked Chuckie.

"I promise," Jennie nodded.

"Okay. Night, night," Chuckie smiled.

Jennie staggered back to her room and slumped into bed. She was asleep in seconds. And then the animals came back. She was nervous, at first, but when they approached her slowly and gathered around her feet, Jennie calmed down. "Hello, Jennie," squeaked the field mouse.

"Hello, Jennie," said the deer, a little louder.

"Hello, Jennie," screeched the barn owl.

"HELLO, JENNIE!" howled the wolf.

Jennie didn't like the looks of this, so she forced her eyes open... and screamed! There — right in front of her face — was a set of white teeth. Jennie jumped, she jerked, and she spilled the false teeth, and the glass that they were in, and the water that was with them all over her bed.

"GRAMMA'S TEETH!" yelled Chuckie. "SCAAARY!" And he laughed and squealed and rolled all over the bed. "WANNAPLAY?"

Jennie didn't know what she wanted to do. Part of her wanted to be angry. But part of her wanted to laugh right along with Chuckie. One thing was certain — she was wide awake now.

"Okay, Chuckie," she surrendered. "Let's play. The first game will be called, 'Sneak Grandma's teeth back into her room.'"

And that's what they did, snickering and giggling all the way. Chuckie almost woke Grandma up, but Jennie managed to clasp her hand over his mouth, just in time.

"Now what?" she said, when they had finished. "What do you want to play next?"

"CARS!" grinned Chuckie, and he grabbed her hand and led her to his bedroom. They dug out a shoebox full of tiny cars, but before even five minutes had passed, Chuckie started to yawn.

"Sleepy," he said. And he crawled up onto his bed. Jennie tucked him in, but as she went to stand up, he grabbed her round the neck and kissed her.

"Cousin Jennie. Best friend," he whispered. Then he let go and curled up under his blanket.

Jennie started back to her room and bed, then remembered the spilt glass of water.

"Oh, well," she sighed as she crawled in beside Chuckiebee.

"Wannagotosleep," she whispered to him. And that's exactly what she did. The whole night through.

Has anything like what happened to Jennie in the story ever happened to you? If it has, did you finally give in to the person who kept asking you for something?

One time, when Jesus was teaching his followers about praying, he told them a story something like this.

This is Jesus' story:

Prayer
(Lk 11:5–10)

"Suppose one of you goes to a friend in the middle of the night and says, 'Let me borrow three loaves of bread. A friend of mine has dropped in, and I don't have a thing for him to eat.' And suppose your friend answers, 'Don't bother me! The door is bolted, and my children and I are in bed. I cannot get up to give you something.'

"He may not get up and give you the bread, just because you are his friend. But he will get up and give you as much as you need, simply because you are not ashamed to keep on asking.

"So I tell you to ask and you will receive, search and you will find, knock and the door will be opened for you. Everyone who asks will receive, everyone who searches will find, and the door will be opened for everyone who knocks."

In this story Jesus teaches us to keep asking God for what we need. God always answers our prayers. Even though God's answer may not be the answer we want or expect, it's always the one that's *best* for us.

97

What did this story teach you about the way you should pray?

PRAY

Jesus, I'm glad you taught us how to pray. Now I know that God is happy when we ask him for all that we need. There are so many good things I want to ask for, for myself, for others and for the whole world!

Poor Michael Much

Based on the Parable of the Rich Fool

When Michael Much turned nine years old,
He looked around his room.
He had everything a boy could want,
Yet his heart was filled with gloom.
A computer game with thirty-two bits,
And all the add-on stuff,
A TV and a VCR, they simply weren't enough!
A boom box and a mountain bike,
Comic books galore.
I've quite a lot,
Thought Michael Much,
But I'd like a whole lot more.

When Michael Much turned seventeen,
He looked around and sighed.
He had everything a boy could want,
But there was something wrong inside.
His sports car and his four-wheel-drive
Were parked out on the street.
A speedboat and a motorbike
Made the set complete.
Expensive clothes and trendy shoes
Were the only things he wore.
I've quite a lot,
Thought Michael Much,
But I'd like a whole lot more.

When Michael Much turned twenty-five,
He looked around his house.
He had everything a man could want,
But he grumbled and he groused.

A jacuzzi and a swimming pool
Weren't enough to make him
    smile.
And there wasn't time for fam-
    ily.
(They would only cramp his
    style.)
His job, career and salary,
That's all he had time for.
I've quite a lot,
Thought Michael Much,
But I'd like a whole lot more.

When Michael Much turned
    forty,
He looked up and down the
    street.
He had everything a man could
    want,
But his life was hardly sweet.
Banks and malls and offices,
He owned them, one and all.
But he had no use for charity
For the sick, or poor, or small.
People and their problems

He chose to just ignore.
I've quite a lot,
Thought Michael Much,
But I'd like a whole lot more.

When Michael Much turned sixty-five,
He threw back his arms and stretched.
He was the richest man in the whole wide world.
It was finally time to rest.

But before he took another breath,
His heart stopped, and he died.
With no family there to mourn him,
It was only God who sighed,
"Love and joy and beauty —
That's what I made you for.
You had a lot,
Poor Michael Much,
But you missed a whole lot more."

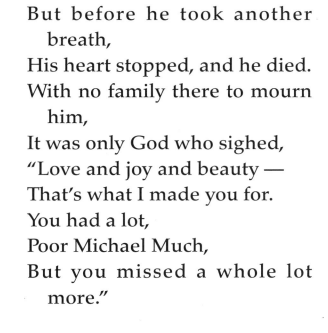

Have you ever been like Michael Much, wanting more things than you really need or can use?

Being greedy and selfish can keep us away from God and from one another.

Here's a story Jesus once told about a greedy and selfish man:

A Rich Fool
(Lk 12:16–21)

LISTEN

"A rich man's farm produced a big crop, and he said to himself, 'What can I do? I don't have a place large enough to store everything.'

"Later, he said, 'Now I know what I'll do. I'll tear down my barns and build bigger ones, where I can store all my grain and other goods. Then I'll say to myself, "You have stored up enough good things to last for years to come. Live it up! Eat, drink, and enjoy yourself."'

"But God said to him, 'You fool! Tonight you will die. Then who will get what you have stored up?'

"This is what happens to people who store up everything for themselves, but are poor in the sight of God."

The rich farmer had much more grain than he could use. What are some things he could have done with the grain instead of hoarding it all for himself?

THINK

In this story Jesus is trying to teach us that life is much more important than *having* a lot of things or money. What matters to God is not how rich we are, but how loving we are.

PRAY

Jesus, I want to be rich in the most important way. I want to be rich in love. Please fill me with your love and help me to share it with everyone I meet.

104

The Place of Honor

Based on the Parable of the Invited Guests

Andrew Whiting could not believe it. He'd heard stories about his great-uncle, Lord Buffington, for years. Stories about his riches and his power and the huge mansion in which he lived. But no one from the poor side of the family had ever been invited to visit. Not until now.

Andrew pinched himself. This was not a dream! It was real! Andrew was actually sitting at his great-uncle's table, surrounded by many wealthy and famous guests. Not only that, he was sitting in the place of honor, next to the great lord himself!

Lord Buffington tapped a silver spoon on the side of a delicate crystal glass. It shivered and chimed a high fine tune right around the dining hall. The guests fell silent.

"Ladies and gentlemen," Lord Buffington wheezed, "I would like to welcome you to my table. This evening..."

But before he could continue, Carstairs, the butler, glided into the room, begged his master's pardon, and whispered something in his ear.

"I'm terribly sorry," Lord Buffington apologized. "A matter of some urgency has arisen. Please carry on. I shall return as soon as possible." With that, he reached for his cane and hobbled out of the room.

The dinner guests were surprised ("How peculiar!"). The dinner guests were curious ("What could be the matter?"). But above all, the dinner guests were *hungry!* The sight and smell of the food got

the better of them, and they began to eat.

Andrew slid his knife through the thickest and most tender piece of beef he had ever seen, and then dipped the meat in a puddle of dark brown gravy. He lifted his fork. Aaaah. And that's when the woman sitting next to Andrew tapped him on the shoulder.

"Pardon me, young man," she gushed. "My name is Lady Agatha Nose-Upton. I wonder if you would mind doing me one teensy little favor?"

Andrew reluctantly put down his fork, "Why, of course," he said. "How can I help?"

"Well," she leaned over and whispered, "I would so like to speak with Lord Buffington this evening. It's been ages since we've talked, and there are one or two little things I should like to discuss with him. Would you mind terribly if we switched places?"

Andrew was more than a little surprised by this request. He had expected her to ask for the salt or something like that. And, to tell the truth, he didn't know how to answer. He was only a boy, after all, and had never been to one of these fancy dinners before. What was the right thing to do? What was the polite thing to do?

Just who am I, anyway? Andrew thought. This is an important lady sitting next to me, but I'm only one of Lord Buffington's poor relatives. She deserves to talk with my uncle more than I do.

"Sure…. All right," Andrew agreed. "We'll swap seats."

"Lovely!" exclaimed Lady Nose-Upton. "You are a dear, sweet young man!"

Andrew blushed. However, he couldn't help noticing the look of disapproval he received from Carstairs as he and the lady exchanged first their plates, then their places.

"A jolly good meal, isn't it?" shouted Andrew's new neighbor.

Andrew picked up his knife and fork. "Well, I, er, really haven't tasted it yet…."

"I'm Colonel Pancake!" said the

man, shouting again as he offered Andrew his hand.

"Pleased to meet you," Andrew said, putting down his fork so he could shake hands with the colonel.

"I was in the war with old Buffy. Why, I could tell you stories that would make your hair stand on end! For example, there was the time we lost our rations and had to survive for an entire week on swamp bugs. Could you pass the potatoes, please?"

Andrew pushed away his plate and reached for the potatoes. This dinner was not turning out as he'd expected.

"I say," Colonel Pancake continued, "Would you think it awfully rude of me to ask if we could trade places? I brought along a few old army pictures, and I'm sure old Buffy would have trouble seeing them at this distance. His eyesight isn't what it was, they say. Why, I remember the time...."

"Yes, yes!" Andrew interrupted, hoping to avoid a story he didn't want to hear. "I don't mind swapping at all."

So once again, plates and seats were rearranged. Carstairs the butler looked very annoyed.

"I'm really sorry about all this switching and swapping," Andrew apologized to the man on his left. "I hope it hasn't upset your dinner."

Upset my dinner, dear boy?" the man whispered. "I've spent the entire meal seated across from Miss Penelope Spigot. What could possibly upset my dinner more than that?"

"I don't know," was Andrew's puzzled reply. "We've never met. What's wrong with her?"

"What's wrong?" gasped the man. "All you have to do is look."

So Andrew looked. And, sure enough, even though Miss Spigot was an attractive young woman, she did indeed have one annoying habit.

"She talks with her mouth full, my lad! Look, there goes a crumb now. And another. Watch out, it's headed this way!" And the man grabbed Andrew by the arm and pulled him under the table.

"The name's Jenkins," he whispered as they rose back into place, "and I know it's asking a lot, but I would so like to be sitting in another spot. I don't suppose we could change places?"

"Why not?" Andrew sighed. It didn't seem that he was going to talk with his uncle at all.

Carstairs the butler glared this time, and was coming toward Andrew when Lord Buffington walked back into the room. Carstairs went to help him to his seat.

Andrew picked at his food and watched as the butler whispered into the old man's ear.

"Oh, well," Andrew sighed. "Looks like I'll be the first and the last Whiting ever to be invited to this place."

Just then, Lord Buffington tapped on his glass again and struggled to his feet. "The reason I have invited you all here tonight is to announce that I'm beginning a new charitable fund for helping those in need. Let's face facts. My family has not always been known for kindness and generosity. But there is one side of the family — the poorer side, I dare say—which has a long history of good works. My great-nephew Andrew, who has joined us here tonight, represents that side. He was to have sat next to me, but it seems that his kindness — or perhaps his humility — has moved him more than a little ways down the table. Andrew, would you come and stand beside me?"

Andrew rose slowly and walked to his great-uncle's side. Every eye in the room was on him. He felt his face grow hot.

Lord Buffington took Andrew's arm. "May I present to you Mr. Andrew Whiting," Lord Buffington announced, "a fine young man who will henceforth be known as the chairman of the Buffington Charitable Fund!"

Andrew couldn't believe it! He was even more surprised when the guests raised their glasses in a toast.

"To Mr. Andrew Whiting!" someone shouted.

"Now then," growled Lord Buffington to the three guests sitting

nearest to him, "I have a great deal to discuss with my nephew. I don't suppose the three of you would mind moving to make room for him?"

"Of course not," mumbled red-faced Lady Nose-Upton.

"Anything you say, Buffington," shouted shaking Colonel Pancake.

"Horrors," muttered Jenkins, as he returned to his seat across from Miss Spigot.

"Dessert, Carstairs," called Lord Buffington. "Dessert here, for my nephew."

"Whatever you say, sir."

And this time, Carstairs the butler smiled.

Andrew was the guest of honor, but he didn't think he was better or more special than the other guests. This means Andrew was humble.

Do you think that Lady Nose-Upton and Colonel Pancake were humble? Why or why not?

One time, Jesus told a story to teach us that we should try to be humble.

This is the story:

How To Be a Guest
(Lk 14:7–11)

LISTEN

Jesus saw how the guests had tried to take the best seats. So he told them:

"When you are invited to a wedding feast, don't sit in the best place. Someone more important may have been invited. Then the one who invited you will come and say, 'Give your place to this other guest!' You will be embarrassed and will have to sit in the worst place.

"When you are invited to be a guest, go and sit in the worst place. Then the one who invited you may come and say, 'My friend, take a better seat!' You will then be honored in front of all the other guests. If you put yourself above others, you will be put down. But if you humble yourself, you will be honored."

THINK

What are some ways that you can be humble at home and at school?

PRAY

Jesus, sometimes I think that I'm better or know more than others do. This can lead me to treat other people in an unkind way. Help me always to be humble like you.

The Best Birthday Party Ever

Based on the Parable of the Banquet

Angie wore the right shoes. She listened to the right music. She had her hair cut just the right way. And when Abbey, Caitlin, and Andrea agreed to come to her twelfth birthday party, she knew she had finally been accepted by the right group.

"But what about Jennifer, up the street?" asked her mom. "You've known her for ages. And your cousin Kelly? And Danielle, from church?"

Angie looked at the ceiling. "Mom," she moaned, "you just don't get it. Abbey, Caitlin, and Andrea are the most popular girls in the entire school!"

"But don't you think your other friends will be hurt that you didn't invite them?"

"Mom!" Angie sighed. "Jennifer and Kelly are only in the fifth grade. They'd feel out of place. And Danielle...well, Danielle is nice and all, but she's kind of *different*, if you know what I mean."

"All right," Angie's mother sighed back. "It's your party. I just don't know any of these popular girls, that's all."

"You'll love them, Mom," Angie smiled. "They're cool."

For the next two weeks, Angie worried and worked and planned. Everything about the party had to be right. Just right. She couldn't afford to mess things up now. Now that she was so close to being a part of the group.

She persuaded her mom to buy a more expensive cake, to make fancier decorations, and to rent a more grown-up video.

"It'll be fine, Mom," she argued. "It's not like we're little kids anymore."

And in between the worry and the work, she dreamed of how impressed her new friends would be, and how she would feel walking through the school halls with them or sharing the latest news on the bus.

When the day of the party arrived, Angie was too excited for words. Saturday was usually her day to sleep in — 'til ten or eleven o'clock. But not this Saturday. She was up at eight, fixing her hair, trying on different outfits, and even cleaning her room! She was just about finished, in fact, when the phone rang.

"Hi, Andrea!" she giggled. But the brightness in her voice didn't last long. "Oh," she said quietly. "No, that's okay. I understand. I mean, what else can you do? Uh-huh. Have a good time."

"Who was that?" called her mother from the kitchen.

"Just Andrea," said Angie. "It's her dad's turn to have her this weekend and he planned a surprise trip. So she can't come to my party."

Oh, dear," her mom said. "Well, that still leaves your other two friends. Why not ask Jennifer or Kelly to take Andrea's place?"

"Mom!" Angie groaned. "I've already explained. They're too young. They won't fit in. We'll still have a great time."

Angie helped her mom finish up the decorations and set the table. That's when the phone rang again.

"I'll get it!" said Angie's mom. But Angie got there first.

"Caitlin! Hi!" she exclaimed. "Did you hear about Andrea? Yeah. You think her dad would have warned her. Well, she's going to be missing a great party! What? What did you say? Can't you just go some other time? Sure…okay…see you."

Angie's mom crept out of the kitchen. "Another cancellation?" she asked.

Angie nodded and started to cry. "Caitlin's cousin called. She lives somewhere out in the country and invited her to go horseback riding."

Angie's mom hugged her. "Well, why can't she go another day?"

"That's what I said," Angie sobbed. "She just got all nasty and said that her cousin never asks her, and this is the only chance she'll probably have all year. Or something like that. Oh, Mom, it's all ruined, and now she's mad at me and I don't know what to do!"

"There are still your other friends," said Angie's mom. But before Angie could answer, the phone rang again.

"Why don't I get it this time?" Angie's mom suggested. "Hello. Yes…I see. Yes, I'll tell her. Thank you for calling."

"It was Abbey, wasn't it?" moaned Angie. "She's not coming, either, is she?"

"No, she's not," her mom answered.

"Did she say why?"

"I don't think you want to know." Angie's mom was obviously angry.

"No, I do. I really do. Is it because of what I said to Caitlin?"

No," her mom replied. "It had nothing to do with Caitlin. It seems that there's this two-hour sale at the mall…."

"The mall!" Angie shouted. "She's missing my party just to go to the mall!?" Now it was her turn to be angry. Angie ran up to her room and slammed the door behind her. She stayed there for more than an hour until a quiet tap interrupted her thoughts.

"Go away."

"I can't." It was her mom. "I need your help with an important decision. There are all kinds of food on the table, some beautiful decorations, and a huge cake. What do you think I should do with them?"

"Throw them away!" came the muffled answer.

"All right," said Angie's mom. "It just seems a shame, that's all — to punish yourself because someone else has hurt you."

There was a long pause.

Angie opened the door a crack. "It *is* my birthday, isn't it?" she said. "So I should have a good time, shouldn't I — even if my friends don't want to come?"

"I think so," said her mother. "And I bet it's still not too late to ask some of your other friends. I mean, you won't have to worry about them not fitting in."

Just for a second, Angie's eyes went to the ceiling. Then she hugged her mom and smiled. "Okay," she nodded. "But will you call them for me?"

As it happens, Kelly and Jennifer and Danielle were more than happy to come. (Danielle even gave up a trip to the mall!) And the party?

"I had a great time!" Angie told her mom later that night.

"So what will you say to your friends? Will you tell them how much they upset you?"

"My friends?" said Angie. "My friends didn't upset me. They came when I needed them. They were here — eating cake and watching a video and making me laugh — at the best birthday party ever!"

Why did Angie invite some of the most popular kids to her party? What did she hope to get out of it?

Once, Jesus went to eat at the home of an important man who had invited him to dinner. Everyone was watching Jesus carefully. Then Jesus told the man a story about how we shouldn't do things only for those who can pay us back.

Here is the story:

Giving a Banquet
(Lk 14:12–14)

"When you give a dinner or a banquet, don't invite your friends and family and relatives and rich neighbors. If you do, they will invite you in return, and you will be paid back. When you give a feast, invite the poor, the crippled, the lame and the blind. They cannot pay you back. But God will bless you and reward you when his people rise from death."

In this story Jesus says that God will reward us for the good things we do for others. He tells us to be kind and loving to other people, especially to those who have more needs. Jesus wants us to do good for others without expecting them to repay us.

What can you do to help someone who is poor, or sick, or lonely? (Hint: Ask your parents for ideas.)

Jesus, I like what you taught us in your story about the banquet. Help me to do good to others without looking for any rewards. I know that I'll get my reward in heaven!

119

Runaway Rabbit

*Based on the Parables of the Lost Sheep,
the Lost Coin, and the Prodigal Son*

It was the same every morning: Carrots and pellets. Pellets and carrots. For Sunny, Sandy, and Sugar. For Cutie, Buttons, and Pete. And, finally, for Duncan's newest rabbits: Wiggles, Fluffy, and...Dot? Where was Dot? Hiding again, probably. Duncan jammed the end of a carrot through the wire mesh wall and jiggled it around.

"Dot," he called. "Here, Dot."

But there was no sign of her black and white nose or her one floppy ear. So Duncan opened up the top of the hutch and clawed through the long grass and hay piled at the back. And that's when he saw the hole — down the back of the hutch, then up and out the other side.

Dot had dug herself a tunnel. Dot was gone!

Duncan ran to tell his mom, but just as he turned the corner for the side door, he bumped into his big brother.

"Watch where you're going, squirt!"

"Sorry," puffed Duncan, all out of breath. "Gotta tell Mom...Dot's gone!"

"Good riddance!" Sean scowled. "She was pretty dumb-looking, anyway."

If Duncan hadn't been in such a hurry, and if his brother hadn't been so big, he would have punched him, right then and there. Duncan liked Dot as much as the rest of his rabbits. Maybe a little more, because she looked so different. But what did Sean know about rabbits, anyway? All he cared about was his stupid garden.

"Look, I've got to tell Mom. I've got to find Dot!" panted Duncan, as he slipped between his brother and the aluminum siding, and shot into the house.

"Well, don't expect me to help!" Sean hollered after him.

Fortunately, Duncan's mother was a lot more understanding. "Tell me when you last saw her," she said.

"Last night, just before bed," answered Duncan. "And she was fine. I take good care of her. Why would she run away?"

"I don't know. But Dot is a lot friskier than your other rabbits. They seem happy just to sit there, but she likes to dig and run and chew."

"She chewed the water bottle up," added Duncan's sister, Molly. "And the dish you put in there. And the wood on the side of her cage. You won't have to worry about that anymore."

"Look," sighed Duncan. "I know she's not the world's most perfect rabbit, but I want her back, okay? And I'll look all by myself, if I have to."

"No, we'll help," promised Duncan's mom. "We'll be happy to, won't we, Molly?"

"Sure," she shrugged. "But you will be in big trouble, Duncan, if that rabbit chews on me!"

They looked in the bushes. They looked in the shrubs. They looked under every tree. And, for the first time, Duncan was sorry his house had such a big yard.

Still looking for that dumb rabbit?" snickered Sean. "I heard the Jacksons' dog barking last night. Maybe he had himself a midnight snack!"

"Stop it!" yelled Duncan.

"Yuck!" groaned Molly.

"That's enough, Sean," their mother warned. "If you won't help, at least you can keep quiet."

"Fine," Sean grunted. "I've got work to do, anyway." And he slung his hoe over his shoulder and headed for the garden. "Hmm," he added, as he disappeared behind the garage. *Dot for Dinner* — it has a nice ring to it!"

"We'll find her!" hollered Duncan. "You'll see!"

"But where?" asked Molly. "We looked everywhere already. Maybe Dot's not in the yard anymore. Or maybe Sean's right."

"Mom! Mom!" Sean shrieked from across the yard. "Get over here, quick! Look at what happened!"

So back they ran—Duncan and his sister and his mom — to Sean's vegetable garden. "Look!" he moaned. "She ate them all! Every single one!"

If a rabbit could smile, then that's what Dot was doing, her cheeks full of fresh young lettuce leaves.

"Dot!" yelled Duncan. He scooped her up and held her tight. "Dot, it's so good to see you!"

Molly and Mom joined in, too, petting and stroking the rabbit and scratching behind her ears. But all Sean could do was fume.

"What about my lettuce? What about all my hard work?" he demanded. "This is all your fault,

Duncan. If your stupid rabbit hadn't escaped, none of this would have happened."

"And if you had helped us look for that rabbit," his mom reminded him, "we might have found her before she had time to gobble down your lettuce. Dot was lost and now we've found her. And I think that calls for a celebration!"

And celebrate they did (well, all but Sean that is). Duncan moved Dot's hutch and filled up the holes, and then filled her food trough with pellets and the nicest carrot he could find.

Meanwhile, his mom cooked up a terrific lunch — ham and baked beans and her Killer Chocolate Brownies for dessert.

Afterwards, Duncan went out to check up on Dot. She had hardly touched the carrot and pellets. She was just lying there, quiet and contented.

"I guess you're still full from before," Duncan said as he reached in and stroked her one floppy ear. And then he smiled. "*Lettuce for Lunch*," he whispered to her. "It has a nice ring to it!"

Have you ever lost something that was very precious to you, as Duncan did in this story? What did you do? How did you feel?

One time, Jesus wanted to tell the people about how happy God is when a person who has sinned turns back to him. Jesus told the people three different stories about how God searches for and welcomes back the "lost" person.

Here they are:

One Sheep
(Lk 15:1–7)

Tax collectors and sinners were all crowding around to listen to Jesus. So the Pharisees and the teachers of the Law of Moses started grumbling, "This man is friendly with sinners. He even eats with them."

Then Jesus told them this story:

"If any of you has a hundred sheep, and one of them gets lost, what will you do? Won't you leave the ninety-nine in the field and go look for the lost sheep until you find it? And when you find it, you will be so glad that you will put it on your shoulders and carry it home. Then you will call in your friends and neighbors and say, 'Let's celebrate! I've found my lost sheep.'"

Jesus said, "In the same way there is more happiness in heaven because of one sinner who turns to God than over ninety-nine good people who don't need to."

One Coin
(Lk 15:8–10)

Jesus told the people another story:

"What will a woman do if she has ten silver coins and loses

one of them? Won't she light a lamp, sweep the floor, and look carefully until she finds it? Then she will call in her friends and neighbors and say, 'Let's celebrate! I've found the coin I lost.'"

Jesus said, "In the same way God's angels are happy when even one person turns to him."

Two Sons
(Lk 15:11–32)

Jesus also told them another story:

"Once a man had two sons. The younger son said to his father, 'Give me my share of the property.' So the father divided his property between his two sons.

"Not long after that, the younger son packed up everything he owned and left for a foreign country, where he wasted all his money in wild living. He had spent everything, when a bad famine spread through that whole land. Soon he had nothing to eat.

"He went to work for a man in that country, and the man sent him out to take care of his pigs. He would have been glad to eat what the pigs were eating, but no one gave him a thing.

"Finally, he came to his senses and said, 'My father's workers have plenty to eat, and here I am, starving to death! I will go to my father and say to him, "Father, I have sinned against God in heaven and against you. I am no longer good enough to be called your son. Treat me like one of your workers."'

"The younger son got up and started back to his father. But when he was still a long way off, his father saw him and felt sorry for him. He ran to his son and hugged and kissed him.

"The son said, 'Father, I have sinned against God in heaven and against you. I am no longer good enough to be called your son.'

"But his father said to the servants, 'Hurry and bring the best clothes and put them on him. Give him a ring for his finger and sandals for his feet. Get the best calf and prepare it, so we can eat and celebrate. This son of mine was dead, but has now come back to life. He was lost and has now been found.' And they began to celebrate.

"The older son had been out in the field. But when he came near the house, he heard the music and dancing. So he called one of the servants over and asked, 'What's going on here?'

"The servant answered, 'Your brother has come home safe and sound, and your father ordered us to kill the best calf.' The older brother got so angry that he would not even go into the house.

"His father came out and begged him to go in. But he said to his father, 'For years I have worked for you like a slave and have always obeyed you. But you have never even given me a little goat, so that I could give a dinner for my friends. This other son of yours wasted your money on prostitutes. And now that he has come home, you ordered the best calf to be killed for a feast.'

"His father replied, 'My son, you are always with me, and everything I have is yours. But we should be glad and celebrate! Your brother was dead, but he is now alive. He was lost and has now been found.'"

In the first story the shepherd who loses one sheep and goes to look for it stands for God. In the second story the woman who searches for her lost coin stands for God. In the third story the father of the two sons stands for God. These stories teach us that God always goes searching for the person who wanders away from him. God loves us so much that he always welcomes us back — no matter what wrong thing we may have done.

Did any of the three stories surprise you? If you answered yes, why did the story or stories surprise you?

We don't know how the story of the two sons ended. What do *you* think happened? Did the older son finally join the party? Or did he stay outside even after his father came out and talked to him? What would *you* have done in his place?

Jesus, thank you for teaching me about God's wonderful love. God is loving and thinking of me even when I'm not loving and thinking of him. I always want to stay close to God!

Money Matters

Based on the Parable of the Dishonest Steward

Daniel had earned ten dollars and he couldn't wait to spend it!

As it happened, his Grandpa was driving into town.

"Grandpa, can I hitch a ride with you?" Daniel asked.

"Sure," Grandpa grinned.

Grandpa's car was old. It had bright chrome bumpers, a hard metal dashboard and seatbelts that only went across your lap. Daniel's dad called it an antique, but Daniel liked sliding across the plastic seat and turning the chunky knobs on the radio.

"So what are you going to do with that money?" Grandpa asked.

That wasn't an easy question to answer.

"I think I'll buy some comic books," Daniel answered. "Or maybe I'll get a snorkel for under-water swimming. I could get some baseball cards. Or...I don't know. There are so many things I want!"

Grandpa piloted the car into the parking lot. He took up two spaces. Shutting off the motor, he turned to Daniel. "See that store over there?" he asked, pointing to the five-and-ten store across the street. "I used to work there, you know. That's where I had my first job. I wasn't much older than you."

Daniel nodded, but kept quiet. He knew his Grandpa had worked there. Grandpa had told him at least a hundred times already.

"And do you know what I did with my first paycheck?" Grandpa asked.

This Daniel didn't know.

"I saved it. That's what I did. I

went to the bank — just down the street — and I opened a savings account — the very same account I use today."

Daniel cringed. He could tell what was coming next.

"If I'd spent the money," Grandpa continued, "it would be gone — wasted on something I probably didn't need. But because I saved what I earned, I could use it later on for more important things — like buying a home, sending your father to college, or helping those folks whose house burned down." Grandpa paused to let this all sink in. "So why don't you let me take you to the bank?" he concluded. "We can use that $10.00 to set up a savings account for you."

"Aw, Grandpa," Daniel moaned, "I just want to spend it — on comic books or baseball cards, or anything!"

"Daniel," Grandpa sighed, "that money's got a hold on you. It's burning a hole in your pocket. It's screaming in your ear, 'Spend me! Spend me!' If you let money take hold of you like that, you're never going to have enough. Come with me. I want to show you something."

Grandpa climbed out of the car. Daniel followed. He had a sick feeling that he was never going to see those comic books.

Grandpa strolled across the street, waving and tipping his cap as he went along. He seemed to know everyone. But when he came to the front of the five-and-ten store, he stopped. He pointed to the sign. "Look carefully at that sign," he told Daniel. "Do you notice anything strange about it?"

By now Daniel was getting aggravated. "I don't know," he mumbled. "Is it crooked? Is something spelled wrong?"

"You're not even looking," Grandpa chuckled. "Look. Look closer."

Daniel looked again. Well, for the first time, really. And he did see something. "There are shapes of letters — different letters — underneath the ones that are up there now."

"That's right!" Grandpa smiled. "And the older letters — the letters underneath — say *Samuel T. Jones & Sons.* How do I know that? Because it was Mr. Jones who gave me that first job!"

"That's great, Grandpa," said Daniel. "Can we go now?"

Of course not," Grandpa answered. "It's really Sam Jones I want to tell you about." Grandpa pointed to a bench in front of the store. "Have a seat."

Why do we have to live in a cute little town with cute little benches? Daniel wondered. *And why can't it just start to rain?*

But nothing was going to stop Grandpa now. He took a deep breath and began to tell his story.

"The owner of this store, Sam Jones, had a partner by the name of Mr. Butler. Mr. Butler paid the bills, counted the money, that sort of thing. Well, one day, Mr. Jones took a look at the accounting records himself. And guess what? He found that Mr. Butler had been stealing from the business. So Mr. Jones called Mr. Butler into his office and ended their partnership.

"I was on the cleaning detail at the time — sweeping, washing the windows, and emptying all the trash — and I happened to overhear Mr. Butler on the phone. He was talking to his wife. 'No, I'm not going to dig ditches,' he said. 'My back won't take it. And no, I'm not going to work for your brother. That would be like taking charity. He'd never let me forget it. No, my dear, I've got a plan.'

The next thing I knew, Mr. Butler started calling everyone who owed Sam Jones money. 'Hank,' he said to the man who ran the bakery, 'you owe fifty dollars. Pay thirty today and your debt is clear.'

"Then he called the butcher. 'Jim,' he said, 'about that eighty dollars you owe, pay us fifty and we'll forget the rest.' By reducing the debts that people owed the store, Mr. Butler was giving away his share of the business.

"On and on he went calling up every business in town offering them these deals. And then, before I could even finish sweeping up, each and every one of the people who owed the store money came running in, cash in hand, to pay the "discount" rates Mr. Butler had given them! 'Thanks, Mr. Butler,' they all said, 'Thanks a lot.'"

Daniel looked puzzled. "What did Mr. Jones do when he found out? I'll bet he was madder than ever."

"You would have thought so," Grandpa nodded, "but it didn't work out that way. Mr. Jones had given up hope that the people would pay him anything at all. So getting back even a part of the money they owed made him hap-pier than a honey bee at a flower show!"

"Did he take Mr. Butler back?" Daniel asked.

"No. He just couldn't trust him. But Mr. Butler had no problem getting work from those fellas whose debts he had lowered. And as far as I know, he never did have to dig a ditch or work for his broth-er-in-law. And that's my point."

What?" asked Daniel, more confused than ever. "Are you saying I should use my money to cheat people?"

"Of course not!" Grandpa exclaimed. "The real point is that Mr. Butler — crooked as the man was — managed to take care of his most important needs for years to come. He knew how to make the most of a situation in order to get what he needed and wanted."

"And all I want is some comic books!" Daniel pleaded. "So can we please go in and buy some?"

"Is that what you *really* want?" asked Grandpa.

"I'm not sure," Daniel sighed. "What if I just spend a little of my money now and think about what to do with the rest?"

Grandpa stood up and smiled. "Sounds good to me," he said, heading for the five-and-ten. "And maybe while we're in here, I can use some of *my* money to get what *I* want."

"What do you want?" Daniel asked.

Grandpa grinned. "Why, two jumbo-sized hot fudge sundaes, of course!"

What did you think about Mr. Butler in this story?

One time, Jesus told a story about some-one like Mr. Butler.

This is Jesus' story:

A Dishonest Manager
(Lk 16:1–13)

"A rich man once had a manager to take care of his busi-ness. But he was told that his manager was wasting money. So the rich man called him in and said, 'What is this I hear about you? Tell me what you have done! You are no longer going to work for me.'

"The manager said to himself, 'What shall I do now that my master is going to fire me? I can't dig ditches, and I'm ashamed to beg. I know what I'll do, so that people will wel-come me into their home after I've lost my job.'

"Then one by one he called in the people who were in debt to his master. He asked the first one, 'How much do you owe my master?'

" 'A hundred barrels of olive oil,' the man answered.

"So the manager said, 'Take your bill and sit down and quickly write "fifty".'

"The manager asked someone else who was in debt to his master, 'How much do you owe?'

" 'A thousand bushels of wheat,' the man replied.

"The manager said, 'Take your bill and write "eight hun-dred".'

138

"The master praised his dishonest manager for looking out for himself so well. That's how it is! The people of this world look out for themselves better than the people who belong to the light.

"My disciples…anyone who is dishonest in little matters will be dishonest in important matters. If you cannot be trusted with this wicked wealth, who will trust you with true wealth? And if you cannot be trusted with what belongs to someone else, who will give you something that will be your own? You cannot be the slave of two masters. You will like one more than the other or be more loyal to one than to the other. You cannot serve God and money."

One thing this story teaches us is that being too greedy for money can cause problems. It can lead us to do things that aren't right. It can even keep us from loving and serving God as we should. Jesus wants us to keep looking for ways to make God first in our lives. What are some things you can do to make God first in your life?

Jesus, money is something that our families need. But God, other people, and the gifts of life and love are even more important! Help me to always remember this.

Andy Lazarus and D. Ives

Based on the Parable of Lazarus and the Rich Man

The school bus crested the hill and knocked an icicle off an overhanging branch. Danny Ives snickered. "Did you two get a whiff of Andy today?"

"Are you kidding?" laughed his friend Mark.

"Yeah," added Brian, squeezing his nose between his fingers. "How could you miss it?"

The bus rolled around a sharp bend, and the three friends turned to look at Andy Lazarus. He was sitting by himself, four seats back.

"Smellorama!" shouted Danny.

"Sir Fume-a-Lot!" added Mark.

"From Stink City!" chuckled Brian.

Andy slumped down in his seat and looked out the window. The winter day shivered past, a blur of blue and white, as he tried hard to hide his wet eyes.

The bus started down a long hill. The temperature dropped. More snow began to fall.

"Well, what do you expect?" said Danny. "You've seen his house."

"Yeah," agreed Mark. "If I lived there, I'd have the bus drop me off somewhere else."

"Like the dump!" joked Brian. And they all laughed again.

There was a turn at the bottom of the hill and the bus driver began to slow down.

"I just wish he'd quit hanging around us," muttered Danny.

"I know," agreed Mark. "It's embarrassing!"

As the driver stepped harder on the breaks, the bus began to skid, then to slide wildly out of control.

"Hey!" yelled Brian. "I think there's something wrong!"

The bus suddenly crashed into a guardrail and tumbled through the snow.

When Danny awoke, all he was aware of was the smell. It wasn't a hospital smell. And it certainly didn't smell like home. It was an awful smell, really...and then he remembered. The bus. The snow. Brian and Mark...and...of course!... Andy Lazarus. It was the *Andy* smell!

But when he opened his eyes, Andy was nowhere to be seen. Brian and Mark were gone too. Danny was alone, on a bed in a dirty, dingy room.

He got up slowly. No broken bones. Not even a bruise. Then he walked carefully to the window and looked through the greasy pane.

The sky was dingy, too. Like night, or almost night. But there was no star or moon. Just pile upon pile of sad gray clouds.

Where am I? thought Danny. But before he could even start to work out an answer, the door behind him burst open, and then a flying bottle whizzed past his head and smashed against the wall beyond.

"What are you doing in here, boy!" growled a voice from the open door. "I told you an hour ago to feed them hens!"

Danny was scared now. He wanted to run, hide, leap back into that bed, dirty as it was, and bury himself in the covers.

"Did you hear me, brat? Are you deaf? Now get out there before I really lose my temper!"

Get out where? And how? Danny wondered. And then he saw the door on the other side of the room. He shot through it to the yard beyond.

Danny ran and ran until he was out of breath, until that mean voice was a distant echo, until the tall fence in front of him would let him run no further. He turned around, slumped against the fence, and looked back to where he'd been. He knew that house. It was Andy's house!

But where had this fence come from? There had never been a fence in front of Andy's house be-

fore. Just a messy yard and the road — the road that led back through town and home!

Danny turned back to the fence. He poked his fingers through the wire and started to climb. But when he got to the top and looked down, there was no road. Only a steep cliff overlooking a deep, dark pit.

Danny Ives swallowed hard and crept back down the fence. Just as his feet touched the ground, he heard a voice.

"Danny! Danny, I'm over here!"

The voice came from the other side of the pit. It was a voice Danny knew.

"Andy! Andy!" he called back. "I'm over here! I'm at your house. Where are you?"

All of a sudden, the dark clouds parted, and Danny saw Andy Lazarus surrounded by sunlight, dressed in clean clothes, standing in Danny's front yard! There was Danny's bike and his scooter and the swing set his little sister used. And there was something or someone else walking slowly toward Andy.

"It's an angel, Danny," called Andy. "I think we're dead."

"But I don't understand," Danny shouted back. "Why am I over here? It's so awful! And why are you at my house?"

The angel put his hand on Andy's shoulder. "When he was alive," the angel explained, "Andy had nothing. His father didn't take good care of him. Andy was poor and sad and lonely. Instead, you and your friends had everything — good homes, loving families, and plenty of toys and games. All Andy wanted from you was friendship. But you made fun of him and were mean to him and only made his life harder. Now Andy will have what he missed. And you will learn what his life was like."

"No! No!" shouted Danny. "I don't want to stay here. I don't want this. Let me come over to you!"

"I'm sorry," said the angel. "You see the pit. There is no way across."

"But what about Brian and Mark?" Danny said. "They made fun of him, too. Why aren't they here?"

"They survived the bus accident," answered the angel.

"But shouldn't somebody warn them that if they don't change they'll end up like Danny someday?" Andy interrupted.

"Yeah!" shouted Danny. "Good idea! I could go back and tell them." Danny looked at the angel. "You can let me go to Mark and Brian, can't you? You're an angel, after all."

"No," sighed the angel, "No, I can't. And besides, they already know the difference between kindness and cruelty. If they don't want to change, what good would it do for someone to talk with them, even if that someone came back from the dead?"

"Please!" cried Danny. "Please let me out of here!" But the more he pleaded, the darker the house across the pit grew. "Please!" he cried one more time. Soon there was only darkness again.

The next light Danny saw was the one above his hospital bed.

T here we are," smiled a nurse. "It's about time you woke up. Your parents have been worried sick. They just stepped out for the phone. I'll go and get them."

"Hey, Danny! I'm glad you're awake!" It was that voice, again. It was that *smell!*

"Is that you, Andy?" whispered Danny. "You're alive?"

"Yeah," chuckled Andy. "I broke some bones. And you had a concussion. But that's all. We're gonna be okay. And we're gonna get to be roommates for awhile!"

"I get it," said Danny. "And am I ever glad!"

In this story, other kids kept away from Andy and made fun of him because he was poor and didn't have all that they had. How do you think this made Andy feel? What are some ways that you can help kids who are left out of games or made fun of at school?

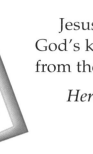

Jesus once told a story about how life in God's kingdom of heaven will be different from the way it is here on earth.

Here is his story:

Lazarus and the Rich Man
(Lk 16:19–31)

LISTEN

"There was once a rich man who wore expensive clothes and every day ate the best food. But a poor beggar named Lazarus was brought to the gate of the rich man's house. He was happy just to eat the scraps that fell from the rich man's table. His body was covered with sores, and dogs kept coming up to lick them. The poor man died, and angels took him to the place of honor next to Abraham.

"The rich man also died and was buried. He went to hell and was suffering terribly. When he looked up and saw Abraham far off, and Lazarus at his side, he said to Abraham, 'Have pity on me! Send Lazarus to dip his finger in water and touch my tongue. I'm suffering terribly in this fire.'

"Abraham answered, 'My friend, remember that while you lived, you had everything good, and Lazarus had everything bad. Now he is happy, and you are in pain. And besides, there is a deep ditch between us, and no one from either side can cross over.'

"But the rich man said, 'Abraham, then please send Lazarus to my father's home. Let him warn my five brothers, so they won't come to this horrible place.'

"Abraham answered, 'Your brothers can read what Moses and the prophets wrote. They should pay attention to that.'

"Then the rich man said, 'No, that's not enough! If only someone from the dead would go to them, they would listen and turn to God.'

"So Abraham said, 'If they won't pay attention to Moses and the prophets, they won't listen even to someone who comes back from the dead.'"

After they died, Lazarus and the rich man got just the opposite of what they had here on earth. One of the things Jesus is trying to teach us in this story is that God wants those who have more to share with those who have less.

THINK

Can you think of some ways that you and your family can help poorer families? Talk about this with your mom and dad. (Hint: You might be able to give clothes you have outgrown to organizations that help families in need. Or you might be able to bring canned food to places that distribute food to homeless people.)

PRAY

Jesus, you have a special love for the poor. Please give me this love too. I want to help those who have less than I. Even the small things I do can make a difference!

Pauline
BOOKS & MEDIA

The Daughters of St. Paul operate book and media centers at the following addresses. Visit, call or write the one nearest you today, or find us on the World Wide Web, www.pauline.org

CALIFORNIA
3908 Sepulveda Blvd, Culver City, CA 90230   310-397-8676
5945 Balboa Avenue, San Diego, CA 92111   858-565-9181
46 Geary Street, San Francisco, CA 94108   415-781-5180

FLORIDA
145 S.W. 107th Avenue, Miami, FL 33174   305-559-6715

HAWAII
1143 Bishop Street, Honolulu, HI 96813   808-521-2731
Neighbor Islands call: 800-259-8463

ILLINOIS
172 North Michigan Avenue, Chicago, IL 60601   312-346-4228

LOUISIANA
4403 Veterans Memorial Blvd, Metairie, LA 70006   504-887-7631

MASSACHUSETTS
Rte. 1, 885 Providence Hwy, Dedham, MA 02026   781-326-5385

MISSOURI
9804 Watson Road, St. Louis, MO 63126   314-965-3512

NEW JERSEY
561 U.S. Route 1, Wick Plaza, Edison, NJ 08817   732-572-1200

NEW YORK
150 East 52nd Street, New York, NY 10022   212-754-1110
78 Fort Place, Staten Island, NY 10301   718-447-5071

OHIO
2105 Ontario Street, Cleveland, OH 44115   216-621-9427

PENNSYLVANIA
9171-A Roosevelt Blvd, Philadelphia, PA 19114   215-676-9494

SOUTH CAROLINA
243 King Street, Charleston, SC 29401   843-577-0175

TENNESSEE
4811 Poplar Avenue, Memphis, TN 38117   901-761-2987

TEXAS
114 Main Plaza, San Antonio, TX 78205   210-224-8101

VIRGIpNIA
1025 King Street, Alexandria, VA 22314   703-549-3806

CANADA
3022 Dufferin Street, Toronto, Ontario, Canada M6B 3T5   416-781-9131
1155 Yonge Street, Toronto, Ontario, Canada M4T 1W2   416-934-3440

¡También somos su fuente para libros, videos y música en español!